T0165185

Spiritual Evolution

How Science Redefines Our Existence

Chad Kennedy, Ph.D.

authorHOUSE®

AuthorHouse™
1663 Liberty Drive
Bloomington, IN 47403
www.authorhouse.com
Phone: 1-800-839-8640

First published by AuthorHouse 1/26/2012

ISBN: 978-1-4670-2414-3 (sc)
ISBN: 978-1-4670-3560-6 (hc)
ISBN: 978-1-4670-2415-0 (e)

Library of Congress Control Number: 2011918198

Printed in the United States of America

Any people depicted in stock imagery provided by Thinkstock are models, and such images are being used for illustrative purposes only. Certain stock imagery © Thinkstock.

This book is printed on acid-free paper.

2011 TechMediaNetwork Inc.SPACE.com image. All rights reserved. Used by permission.

Cover was designed by Maja Tatar

TABLE OF CONTENTS

ACKNOWLEDGMENT

First and foremost, this book would have never been realized if it were not for the love and understanding of my wife, Renea, and children, Lucas, Roland and Talin. They make me a better human being and ground me in the great joys of life. Also thank you to my parents and siblings for their love, for believing in my offbeat ideas and for allowing me to spiritually grow in my own way. To my grandparents, who I feel are still watching now, thank you for never giving up on me and setting high standards of character and integrity.

I would also like to thank my entire first round of editors and reviewers, Jeff Bade, Jim Gerow, Jack Kennedy and Bill Wootton. You were willing to read through my rough drafts and give me constructive feedback (without laughing too hard). Your efforts helped create an overall better and more understandable work out of some very difficult material.

To Teri Watkins and the entire Team Tiber, my publishing team, thank you for all of your help in putting together the book design and getting the book onto the shelves. A special thank you to Professor Maja Tatar for creating book cover design. Also thanks to Jason Poole my web designer for creating and educating me on the finer points of website management. Finally to the reader, thank you for taking the leap of faith to purchase this work, I hope you enjoy it.

PROLOGUE-WHY THIS BOOK? WHY NOW?

*-In this century we have made remarkable material progress,
but basically we are the same as we were thousands of
years ago. Our spiritual needs are still very great.-*

-Tenzin Gyatso, 14th Dalai Lama

My hope is that readers of this work will find greater happiness and fulfillment in the miracle we call life. My purpose for writing this book is to convey a profound realization that modern knowledge and science must be integrated with the spiritual aspect of human lives if we are to have the will and ability to spiritually evolve, or 'Spiritual Evolution'. Despite institutional pressures to remain separate domains of human understanding, we as human beings don't experience nature and life as separate. This experiential paradox occurs within all of us, and perhaps has caused tremendous amounts of human confusion, pain and suffering.

When undertaking a book like this, I place a great deal of thought, care and effort to being sensitive to multiple points of view. In addition, my intent is to use scientific discovery and knowledge to develop the spiritual argument, while keeping the content accessible to non-scientifically trained readers. The hope is that anyone can read this work and reap the benefits of knowledge that is typically only available in scientific journals riddled with unintelligible jargon to the layperson. So with this purpose in mind, let me explain why I feel this book had to be written now.

The simple answer is there is no better time than the present. For the present is *all* we truly perceive. The long answer lies within recent events, surrounding passionate hate rhetoric arising in politics, religion and science. I feel that humanity is fundamentally and uniformly out of balance and looking for clarity. The recent assassination attempt of Arizona Congresswoman, Democratic House Representative Gabrielle Gifford, raised national awareness and debate of anger and intolerant fervor brewing below the surface of normal human behavior. Before we can even begin to understand the source of such discontent and deplorable actions, we need to turn back the arrow of time and reexamine a bit of how we got here.

Historically, human beings vacillate around or on concepts of the "meaning of life", yet in all of history we have never come to such a crossroad of indecision, regarding spirituality and science, as we are now. Throughout this text, we will explore some of the reasons for how we got here.

In Greece, during Aristotle's time (384-322 BCE), the idea of separating questions of existence, meaning and creation from fundamental logic and science was preposterous (1). As mainstream spirituality became virtually synonymous with religious belief, the rifts between existing polytheistic belief systems created much of the hostility that lead to early wars. By the 4th century CE[1] the major monotheistic religions were taking hold in the Roman Empire, and the divide grew even bigger as each vied to be the true legitimate religion (2). By the 6th century CE, the simple act of questioning major religions, such as Catholicism, via science or logic, was enough to get you condemned, arrested or even killed by tribunals. The most infamous tribunal, started in the 15th century CE, was the Spanish Inquisition (3), (4).

The monotheistic institutions such as Catholicism, Islam and Judaism are not necessarily to blame for desiring to preserve themselves at perilous or sometimes immoral costs, for that is the innate impulse for most entities particularly in nature. I hypothesize that any emergent entity of sufficient complexity, once born into existence, behaves like a living organism. Through case studies we shall discover governments, corporations, religious institutions and all 'life' in general aim to survive, grow and persist, sometimes at dire costs.

Historically and now, the great monotheistic religions fight not only for institutional, spiritual and moral superiority over each other, but also over common people (2). Whether unintentional or intentional by those in power positions within religious structures, institutions wield various weapons to ensure survival. Weapons of mass deception at their disposal are 'holy' writings (many of which have been terribly altered from originals), lack of education of common folk and the primary weapon, *fear*. Fear, that if one does not follow the path and support the very institution dolling out it's

---

I am using the CE or "Common Era" convention for calendar dates to promote spiritual neutrality and not promote any particular faith or viewpoint.

"teachings and guidance", life and potentially afterlife is at risk or at most eternally damnable (5) (6).

It was not until the brave few, understandably in private, began questioning the most basic assumptions behind religious dogma. Is the world flat? Are we really the center of the cosmos? Is there more?

Breakthroughs in the early scientific age were as profound as their ancient Greek and Arabic philosophic predecessors who brought us the Archimedes principle of buoyancy and Algebra, respectively. Calculations of celestial body movements by Copernicus were published in his work *De Revolutionibus Orbium Caelestium* in 1543 CE which reestablished a heliocentric or (sun centered) model of the universe (7). Galileo later observed and confirmed Copernicus's basic ideas in the 1600s. So repeatable and convincing was Galileo's work that soon the consensus of learned and influential institutions, namely the Universities founded in the Christian dominated West around 1200 CE, forced religious powers to reconcile and accept a heliocentric Copernican model of the known cosmos instead of the Aristotle and Ptolemaic geocentric (earth centric) model (8) (9).

This deeper understanding of our solar system did not emerge overnight. In fact, in 1633 CE the Roman Catholic Inquisition tried and found Galileo guilty of heresy for his role in promoting the heliocentric model and sentenced him to house arrest. There Galileo stayed until he died in 1642 at his home in Florence, Italy. It was not until 1758, over 100 years after Galileo had passed away, that the Catholic Church dropped the general prohibition of books advocating heliocentrism. Furthermore, it was not until 1822 by decree of the Sacred Congregation of the Inquisition, with approval by Pope Pius VII, that the Catholic Church modified their "official" opinion (a.k.a. divine interpretation) of these findings and allowed printing of heliocentric books (10). Acceptance took close to 200 years. Better late than never!

Surprisingly, in complete historical ignorance and lack of any true scientific evidence, fringe, ultra-fundamentalist religious factions continue to refuse collective evidence. A particular group, called Catholic Apologetics International (CAI), uses questionable credentials and propagate misinformation in regards to geocentrism (11) (12). Although groups like these have contradicting opinions to heliocentrism, I still feel fortunate to live in a country with spiritual freedom that allows dissenting views. For in this environment, we can also discover emergent research, explore the unknown and challenge the assumptions and dogma of our predecessors. Not for the purpose of throwing away the old, but rather to elaborate or develop a more inclusive understanding of the Universe in which we live. Therefore, citizens of free countries need to treat this freedom of expression with great responsibility and integrity. We should not abuse our freedoms in favor of egocentrism, self righteousness or greed, lest we lose the very freedom which allows for open discourse.

There are still many countries such as Burma, China, Afghanistan, North Korea and others where heretics are arrested, tortured, exiled or even killed for open spiritual thinking depending upon the laws of the country (13). Even in the United States, where we pride ourselves on spiritual freedom, there are those who would accuse me of blasphemy for questioning traditional spiritual practice, because they are taught not to question spiritual authority. This brings up an excellent question. Who has spiritual authority? A priest? A bishop? A prophet? A Mosque? A Church? You? Me? None of the above? Keep these questions in mind as we venture deeper down the rabbit hole of discovery.

With heightened knowledge and new discoveries presenting themselves almost daily, we are more capable now than at any other time in history to reconcile some of our biggest questions and assumptions about spirituality and its interplay with logic. Many people are looking into more fascinating questions of existence than ever before. Does this mean we can relinquish all personal responsibility to explore and grow with confidence that all will be taken care of; and thus, we have nothing to contribute as individuals? Absolutely not! Why? The reason is, as knowledge progresses forward, resistant forces that wish to maintain the status quo, are unwittingly working to undermine the next emergent event of human kind, namely mass spiritual evolution. I am not speaking of devilish figureheads bent on oppression, as with the long forgotten institutions of old. What I am suggesting is that resistance to human spiritual transformation occurs through *any entity that fights for its continued existence and growth by the fundamental requirement to keep or control the spiritual status quo.*

The previous statement may seem like a dichotomy, but as we explore how discovery and thought uncover new realms of complexity, spirituality, quantum physics, relativity, mathematics, logic, neuroscience, biology, astrophysics, meditation, universal systems, genetics, agent based computation and philosophy, we will discover an underlying common truth so profound that we as a species may never be able to return to a way of purely consumption based existence.

Perhaps by exploring together, the spark of enlightenment may begin with this conversation and start a cascade of events that will forever change 'The Way' of humankind towards a new Way of existence. The Way is traditionally an Eastern phrase which has several meanings synonymous with 'The Path' or 'The Enlightened Road.' The following paradoxical Koan from Zen Master Mumon perhaps better explains 'The Way'.

> *A master was asked the question 'What is the Way?' by a curious monk.*
>
> *'It is right before your eyes,' said the master.*
>
> *'Why do I not see it for myself?'*
>
> *'Because you are thinking of yourself.'*
>
> *'So long as you see double, saying "I do not" and "you do," and so on, your eyes are clouded,' said the master.*
>
> *'When there is neither "I" nor "you," can one see it?'*
>
> *'When there is neither "I" nor "you," who is the one that wants to see it?'*
>
> *-Koan of Zen Master Mumon (13th century)*

I want to be clear. Although I personally ascribe to a form of divine influence on life and that life has infinite potential, I do not believe in a solitary human as 'The' prophet, second coming or witness as a requirement. *That being said, we are all beings with far more grace and potential than we now practice, and for that there is something truly inspiring and mysterious about our collective future.* Lastly, I do believe a true enlightenment journey combined with exploration into the divine Universe is possible for all aware, sentient species.

To begin, we will reexamine some early teachings that govern how we individually 'see' reality. I now challenge you to open your mind to a reality in which science and spirituality, together, can reveal unexpected and exhilarating answers. Alas, as with all great wisdom, more answers beg more questions.

PART I:

BREAKING DOWN PERSONAL SPIRITUAL BARRIERS

CHAPTER 1
EARLY TEACHINGS

-If the truth of everything has already been defined by those that came before us; the very existence of the unknown Universe would be an awful waste of time and space-

IN THE BEGINNING

From the time we are born through the time of our earliest life teachings (typically from our parents, youth pastors, clergy, rabbis, clerics, schools, etc...), we are given a template, a starter set of instructions, if you will, from those that most directly have a vested interest in how and what we think. While the 'rules' are often given with the best of intentions, we as children are vaguely aware that we are being compelled toward some form of group compliance. In plain words, we are being told what to believe, how to fit in, how to live, and how to die. All of these are predefined by our local culture, religion and society.

The indoctrination of individuals depends extraordinarily upon whom you were born to, what geographic region you live in and what level of personal liberty exists during the time in which you come into this life. We initially comply with this indoctrination due to our innocence, naivety and desire to please. As children we did not have the wisdom, will or evidence to challenge our parents and culture. Therefore, for better or worse, we were easily shaped and molded by the ideals of our caregivers.

Much of what is taught is sound advice, such as "thou shalt not kill" and the like. Such basic wisdom for living and getting along with others is fairly common to the World's current religions. It is in the minutia and literal extremes where failure of peaceful coexistence arises. We may ask ourselves during adolescence, 'Why is this so?', 'Why do we believe our way and our neighbors another way?' or 'What makes our belief right?' Unfortunately, for most of us, our questions are charged as insubordination, a challenge to authority, blasphemy or faithless. As a result, our thoughts are persecuted in one of the following ways.

1. Who are we to question those who have preceded us?
2. Have you no respect for the teachings presented?
3. Who do you think you are? (Great question by the way!)
4. Or the most terrifying of all, the dreaded paraphrase, "If you do not believe in the word of <insert name of deity, saint or prophet here> purely on faith, you are unworthy of the holy kingdom of eternal 'good' life and will forever (burn, freeze, be tortured or insert the suffering of choice) in eternal damnation."

Honestly, what is a young mind to do with the last ultimatum, such an obvious threat, especially with little to now access to credible information or proof? If today's religious doctrines were held to the same academic standards that most science is held to today, it is seriously doubtful that many ideas could pass muster. Add to this the seemingly incoherent global messages and news bombarding our youth today and it is no wonder that most teens and adults alike have astonishingly high levels of anxiety, fear and stress in this day and age.

As parents and adults we ask ourselves, 'Why do kids today seem so directionless, rebellious, lost or in extreme cases suicidal?' Not all, but part of that may be because of the contrary messages they receive. Kids are taught to preserve, believe in, and cherish their particular brand of *spirituality* (commonly confused with religion), above others. The fundamental act of distinguishing one's religion as above another, by definition, creates separation. We create an illusory mental model in our subconscious mind that pits 'us against them', thus separating our 'community' of 'being' from others.

There are positive effects of organized religion. For instance, religious institutions provide a sense of community. Abraham Maslow's hierarchy of need discusses a sense of belonging and safety as basic human needs that must be met to achieve happiness. Although various organized religions provide that sense of community it often comes at a very high price, can be fickle or all together an illusion. Members only belong if they conform to the consensus of belief. The moment that belief is challenged, the illusion disappears, and what remains is condemnation, rejection or outright exile. In the dark ages this was the practice of noble fiefdoms.

However, good works of many organized groups include helping with the rearing of families, feeding those in need and giving aid to those less fortunate. Acts of compassion like these are to be commended and encouraged. Just be aware what the cost is versus the value. What is the price you pay?

Negative consequences of institutionalized religion are often feelings of imposing pressure, the sense that everything has been thought through already and there is nothing new to learn or solve in the area of existence. People chronically suffer from ignorance, stifling views and fear of anything outside their defined domain. All too often, these fears express themselves in higher levels of human suffering such as wrongful and immoral persecution of "non-believers", hate crimes, religious war and ethnic execution deemed as "cleansing". There is not a more deplorable or more self-destructive business than destroying all others who don't agree with you. These dangers are exceedingly unsustainable in modern day where mankind has the technological capability, not only destroy our entire human race if we react as segregated fiefdoms, but also all living creatures on the surface of our planet.

Most of this feeling of separation appears in tradition Western religions. Learning a lesson from Eastern traditions such as Buddhism, teaches compassion for all sentient beings. Perhaps we can apply this sense of connectedness. **One way to successfully navigate through this maze of hatred is by embracing our similarities. We need to let go of our differences and jointly discover a new level of spirituality, humanity and compassion that is inclusive of one another rather than exclusive.**

THE "RULES"

-It is important to learn the rules. Then you not only know when to apply them, but most importantly when they don't apply-

Early in our lifetime, we are taught the "Rules". How these rules came about, or the flavor in which they are delivered to our consciousness, varies with each individual. Regardless of the source, societies, religions or nationalities, the "Rules" distill down to a distinctive list. Although not the definitive or exclusive list, it encompasses the basic rules that cross religion, cultural, nationality and time barriers. Here is the major top ten list of "Rules" learned in childhood:

1. Do not kill or harm.
2. If you need to kill or harm, make sure they belong to some "other" group, not "ours.
3. 'We' are good and 'they' are different. (a.k.a. Bad)
4. Those who came before 'us' know what is best for 'us'.
5. Do not steal or covet what others have.
6. 'We' are right and 'they' are ignorant of the truth (a.k.a. wrong)
7. The Divine Source, (God, Allah, Jehovah, Jesus Christ, Zeus and so on), favors 'us' over 'them'.
8. 'Our' holy writings (Bible, Quran, Torah, 道德經, Bhagavad Gītā and others) are holier; and therefore, a more accurate truth than everyone else's.
9. Spread 'our' 'Word' to others and give donations to aid 'us' since 'we' know what is best.
10. Do NOT question or challenge the Rules even if they conflict with observation!

Put in the generalized context and void of any specific religious dogma, some of the rules sound reasonable and appealing, while others appear downright appalling. Most importantly, we need to discriminate between true wisdom, and clandestinely motivated rules. By this, I mean we need to weed out the faulty motivations of particular special interest groups versus our collective global teachings that seem to transcend our human existence and perspective.

FEAR QUESTIONING OF RULES

"The only thing we have to fear is, fear itself"

-*"Franklin D. Roosevelt -1st Inaugural Address"*

Notice the irony, that the very questioning, the point of examining and analyzing the rules, violates rule #10. Thus, many of our thoughts are controlled at an early age by the most fundamental of control levers, fear. Since the dawn of humankind fear has been used, rightly or wrongly, to encourage or discourage certain behavior or thinking. From this point on, I ask you to have the courage and will to question the rules given to you by generations of man. It *is* OK to question and I encourage you to search behind the rules.

Remember the 'telephone' game? In the 'telephone' game of our childhood, someone starts off the game with an intended saying (original oratory) and whispers it into the ear of the person sitting next to them. The saying is then passed onto the next person and the next via the same whisper technique until it comes to the last person who says what they think the original person said. The game usually results in a big laugh for everyone since the message is completely distorted may not even resemble the original message. Similarly, original messages imparted by wise people throughout the ages are significantly distorted and altered by millennia of interpretations, manipulations and misguided understandings.

How can we then assume that a message or rule we are being taught now is the original message of wisdom from someone long ago? We have writings, but very few if any original copies exist from the original orators or authors. Therefore, it is sufficient to surmise that the rules, as presented today, require us to not only question without fear, but also look at the underlying assumptions with fresh perspectives, so that we can attempt to uncover the original wisdom, knowledge and understanding in terms of modern day humanity. However, this is not what many entities want free-thinking people to do, and for good reason; it threatens their existence.

Throughout the ages and even today many facets of religions, governments, charismatic leaders and even corporate entities manipulate the lever of fear for various gains. Not all intentions are for nefarious reasons, but the lever of fear is particularly strong in the spiritual realm, since the lack of scientific evidence in this area of study makes it a prime target for creative license particularly for the opportunistic minded. As a colleague of mine put it, "Are we to believe that Jesus buried all of those million year old dinosaur bones?"

Ultimately the fundamental situation comes down to this, if we are to progress as a species, we need to look beyond the fear and open ourselves up to the possibility of something greater. A Universe, a reality greater than our ancestors knew due to their limited perspectives and understanding. Progress has shown that many of our predecessors were not correct on the physical aspects of existence, so why not the spiritual? A textbook example is quickly learned in science or engineering training is that Newton's Law of gravity is not completely right. Force (F) being equal to the mass (m) of an object multiplied by its acceleration (a), $F = ma$, is simple and elegant. Yet with all of the concrete evidence given to the relationship, along comes a young mathematician/physicist named Albert Einstein, who opens up a relative can of worms. He has the audacity to start questioning the great Newton's assumptions and rules. As Einstein's calculations show, force among other things, is also governed by a small yet profound limitation, the speed of light. This suggests an upper boundary for the acceleration of mass. For example, a theoretical bullet accelerated by magnets in an infinite barrel would never be able to meet or exceed the speed of light.

Despite the massive conflict and disruption this new theory caused in the physics community, Einstein's Theory of Relativity slowly but eventually took off. Furthermore, it was not definitively proved with experimentation, until sometime later. The Relativity concept redefined the way physicists, astrophysicists, mathematicians and engineers viewed our Universe.

The story does not stop there. Even today there are physicists, computational mathematicians, quantum mechanics theorists and research engineers challenging Einstein's theory in new ways. M-theory, faster than light speed theories, entanglement theory, black holes, interacting multiverses, universality, complexity, emergence, noetic science, causality networks, atomic resonance theories and quantum communication are all concepts that stretch our idea of reality to new boundaries. All of this new evidence and information colliding with previous dogmatic assumptions creates a raw primordial soup of ideas just waiting to coalesce into new forms of knowledge.

The edge of knowledge lies before us. Although it appears that there is no clear path across the chasm, piercing the fog of doubt we see the hints, the evidence of light coming from a new higher vantage point from which to see the Universe ahead of us. We must take the leap to find the way forward, because it is there. Some are already stepping out toward the unknown. Others recoil from fear. I challenge you, knowing where the road behind you has repeatedly led, to try something extraordinary and read on.

CHAPTER 2
CONFLICT

-Conflict arises from the illusion of outside barriers. By realizing the barriers are phantasms of your own making, the conflict disappears-

TESTING BOUNDARIES

Without the innate drive to push the boundaries, an 8 month old baby would never progress to be a toddler. A two-to-three year old would never learn to refrain from touching a hot stove, or perhaps, my twins would not have taken out two dozen eggs to hear the sound the shells make as they crunch on the kitchen floor. These are simple life transitions that we take for granted and label 'early childhood development'.

But what about adult development, humankind development and spiritual development, where are these today? Humans would not have populated the known World if we had not had motivated individuals keenly attuned to this sense of curiosity and adventure. Those people who wished to find where the land of the known stops and the mysteries of the oceans begin drove us toward the future we take for granted today. Without this instinctual drive to explore and survive, our genetic ancestor's would have never left northern Africa some 60,000 years ago, and certainly would not have expanded across the continents through the Arctic Circle and back down through North America. How do we know this? The Human Genographic Project, a research project partnership by National Geographic and IBM with non-profit funding from the

Waitt Family Foundation, has proven that all modern humans have genetic footprints in our DNA that can be traced to a small African population. From their genetic pathways, all human migration is traced (14).

Drawing upon a genetically instinctual sense of courage and curiosity, we need to cultivate one more principle, openness. Openness may seem trite and obvious, but most people who have conformed to a way of thinking for an extended period of time create habits, and habits, particularly of opinion, are hard to break.

No one is immune to the draw of the "comfort zone" way of thinking. Once you have a habit that works for you. Why change right? Wrong! Research shows, in populations and species, that the most adaptable incarnations, such as modern humanity's Homo erectus ancestors, survive (15). The ones who cannot change with the surrounding environment become extinct and die such as the Neanderthals.

Interestingly, a similar 'survival of the most adaptable' rule is true for the mind. Individuals whose brains continually adapt have the highest likelihood of fending off debilitating diseases that afflict the brain, such as Alzheimer's, and survive longer after the loss of loved ones. According to the Society for Neuroscience (SFN), decades of research into the degenerative processes of Alzheimer's disease shows that by continually stimulating the brain in new ways, (e.g. physical exercise, mental exercises, enriched environment and new experiences) there is continued re-networking of the neurons, a process called plasticity (16). The non-neuroscience term for plasticity is adaptability. It is the ability of neurons to change their interconnections with one another thus, continuously recreating a new network structure and function. What does that mean to the rest of us who are not neuroscientists by trade? It means that the more you stimulate your brain in novel ways, the more your brain will internally create new connections and redirect old ones to adapt to new conditions. Not only will the brain structure change, but also it also can route signals around say an Alzheimer's disease 'traffic jam', where the brain is impaired. Brain adaptability is analogous to taking new surface streets or expressways built around a 26 car pileup in your 'neuro-interstate highway'.

Similarly, in the business world, many are familiar with large corporations losing their competitive advantage because smaller, more nimble (adaptable) players can move faster to act on new markets and demands. This is why there will always be new entrepreneurs and companies that seem to come out of nowhere, such as Google, Netflix and Facebook, which either take over a market or create a new one. This again is another facet of the same phenomenon. How are these seemingly different phenomena related? They are all Complex Adaptive Systems or CAS (17). We will look more deeply into what a CAS is in later chapters. For now the essence of the message here is that it is in everyone's best interest to remain nimble and flexible in body, mind and spirit.

How do we accomplish this continuous adaptability as individual minds? As a species? As a planet? The answer lies within one simple idea, *possibility*!

When you ask a 3 to 5 year old what they want to be when they grow up what are common answers, "Astronaut, dancer, movie star, fireman, police officer, artist, fighter pilot, explorer, etc?" How often do we hear, "insurance underwriter, telemarketer, sales person, accountant?" Unless they have a parent in those professions, chances are, never. Not to offend, or degrade the value of those professions, but children at that age typically have **no idea** what those professions are and don't have a glimpse of what they would be doing. Furthermore, kids at that age are attracted to what appears to be the most exciting or glamorous professions they are exposed to. Their realm of what is "possible" to be when they grow up is limited only by what they see, hear, and know. Ask some preschoolers and note the answers. Notice that in their answers, there is little thought about how much money they would be making or the political prestige; the choice is about what sounds fun, exciting or meaningful.

As we learn and grow, several things happen to us that change our "realm of possibility". By the age of 5, most children have learned social rules; share, don't hit, (bite, punch or harm) and wait your turn. At this age, many of us also just began learning the "rules" from Chapter 1 via parents, social, educational or religious structures. Throughout adolescence the "rules" get reinforced to the level of indoctrination for many. These kinds of teachings alter some of the child's original idea of what is "possible" in *expanding* and *contracting* ways.

An *expanding possibility* example is a child learning about the existence of stars, moons and planets. Therefore, the child expands their understanding of the Universe. This revelation may inspire new profession possibilities for that child, such as astronomer, astrophysicist, scientist, aerospace engineer, planetologist, astrobiologist or another explorer type.

An example of a *contracting possibility* is teaching a young child that "their" religion believes that the world is the center of the Universe ignoring any evidence to the contrary. The child then takes the information at face value and nullifies any idea of the existence of anything else outside of this artificial boundary placed upon him or her.

Let's expand this notion by examining the geocentric (Earth centered) model. Read the quote below by the German priest and scholar Martin Luther. This is the same Martin Luther who started the Protestant Reformation, the predecessor to modern day Lutherans, created a German translation of the Bible and championed a theology that challenged Papal authority at the expense of his own excommunication (18) (19).

> *'This fool wishes to reverse the entire science of astronomy; but the sacred scripture tells us that Joshua commanded the sun to stand still, not the earth.'*
>
> — *Martin Luther, 1540*

As seen above, Martin Luther taught a stricter reading of the Bible and had this to say about Nicholaus Copernicus's proposed heliocentric (Sun centered) theory used today. In present day, the majority of educated people would think this argument laughable, because humankind has since discovered mountains of evidence that counters the Earth being the center of the Universe, yet not long ago in human history and even today, there are still people trying to propagate these ideas. The Geocentric Bible Foundation of Hugoton, Texas (now defunct) or Catholic Apologetics International (CAI) claim that "Galileo Was Wrong" and that the Earth does not revolve around the Sun (11). In fact the CAI just had their first, that is right, first Annual Catholic Conference on Geocentrism on November 6th, 2010 in Indiana.

Seek knowledge that expands *possibility* instead of contracts *possibility*. **Nothing** is impossible; there are **only** conditional impossibilities! What do I mean by this? I mean that something that may seem impossible under certain conditions, does not dictate the possibility of that same feat under all conditions or circumstances. It may seem impossible by humankind's current understanding, science and technology, but eventually, by flexing our ingenuity, applying diligence and adding a dose of courage, we can create conditions that will allow the impossible (magic→science fiction) to become not only possible (science fiction→science) but probable and commonplace (science→technology). Notice the theme and source of the following quotes:

> *'There is not the slightest indication that energy will ever be obtainable. It would mean that the atom would have to be shattered at will.'*
>
> — *Albert Einstein, 1932*

> *'With regard to the electric light, much has been said for and against it, but I think I may say without contradiction that when the Paris Exhibition closes, electric light will close with it, and no more will be heard of it.'*
>
> — *Erasmus Wilson, Oxford University professor, 1878*

> *'I have not the smallest molecule of faith in aerial navigation other than ballooning.'*
>
> — *Lord Kelvin, President of Royal Society, 1890*

> *'Man will never reach the moon, regardless of all the future scientific advances.'*
>
> — *Lee DeForest (inventor of vacuum tube/electronic valve), 1957*

All of these people were intelligent if not geniuses in their time and all fell prey to the limitations of personal foresight. All of us are vulnerable to making this same mistake, but remember what you think is a fantasy or magic today, may in fact, become the reality of tomorrow.

A great example of a conditional impossibility is the force of gravity. For millennia up through Sir Isaac Newton's time, gravity was seen as a constant force of nature. The quote, "What goes up, must come down..." is a primary example of the common wisdom shared by humans at the time. For the most part, this dogma still holds true for our daily activities. However, if you change the conditions, say accelerate beyond what we call, *"escape velocity"*, you cannot only leave spherical planet we call Earth, but even place yourself in a continuous falling orbit around it. This orbital path is so high, that an object can effectively fall around the earth for years before coming back down (See Figure 1, below) as did Skylab on July 12, 1979 (20). In this environment, we experience what is called microgravity or 'zero G'.

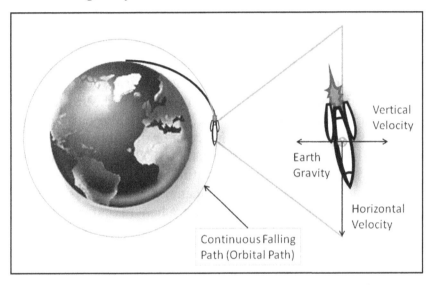

Figure 1: The field of Orbital Mechanics used by NASA and all space agencies operate on basic Newtonian principles of gravity attraction between two objects. In order to achieve orbit a rocket must achieve a high enough vertical velocity to "escape" from the earth's gravitational pull. A sustainable orbit can be achieved placing the rocket into relative "free fall". If we want an object (rocket, space station or satellite) to maintain that orbit, periodic fuel is spent to offset Earth's gravity. If the object runs out of fuel, over a long period of time the object will return to earth as did the Skylab space station on July 12 1979 (20).

Here our notion of what is impossible to do on the surface of the Earth has changed because everything is falling at the same rate so the astronaut's juice can float out of a juice packet to his or her mouth without ever spilling a drop. Of course you don't have to leave the planet to get the microgravity sensation; you can go to any amusement park with a vertical drop ride, set a penny in your hand and watch it float in the air in front of you as you fall. The above example is simplified and not unique. Another way to physically make something defy gravity's pull or 'levitate' can also be accomplished with superconducting magnetic fields. The point is that if we change conditions, things that we perceived as once impossible become not only possible, but probable.

Here is an exercise for you. Make a list of things have you been taught from an early age that you took on faith rather than evidence? Are there stories that sound just as improbable that you were taught (or are still being taught) that you can research independently from your original source? I challenge you to make a top ten list of things that you have always believed, but have never really looked into in an objective manner. Take time to research them one at a time using credible sources (i.e. university libraries, peer reviewed journals and research institutes) and see what the status is on your list of beliefs. What do you find? Are there alternatives ideas or theories that you have never heard of or thought about before? Does this change your perspective of the world around you in some profound way? What are the implications?

Once you are open to the idea that anything is possible, with the right conditions, you need one more ingredient to confronting what holds most of us back from adapting and searching, <u>courage</u>.

FEAR NOT THE QUESTIONING OF RULES

> *"Religion is the masterpiece of the art of animal training,*
> *for it trains people as to how they shall think."*
>
> *- Arthur Schopenhauer, German Philosopher (1788-1860)*

Once you have the courage and the idea that something is possible, the rest is simply the will to follow through. How does one find the courage? How do you turn off, possibly years, of dogmatic programming? The answer is probably a unique one for each of us.

For me personally, the answer came in the form of a series of mini-crises of the heart. I term the experiences as a mini-crisis, since looking back, the actual circumstances seem rather trite, but at the time, from the perspective of a grade school aged child they appeared monumental. These experiences built a nucleus of doubt and questioning that sparked a lifetime of study and inquiry that eventually led me toward the path of mechanical engineering and eventually biomedical engineering research.

My parents had initially baptized me in a catholic church, and for years I followed them as an on again, off again Catholic. As a child, I remember participating in all the various forms of repetitive and seemingly meaningless rituals, where I had no clue what was being said, what was happening or why. The majority of rituals and hymns performed were in Latin, which was, needless to say, not my second or even third language.

Later as my parents, mostly my father, drifted from the Catholic Church, in his own search for a form of worship that resonated with he and my mother, we started attending some other Christian based churches ranging from Presbyterian, Protestant and Non-denominational churches. Ironically, what they settled on had less to do with the type of religion practiced as it did with the warmth of the community that they felt with the Preacher and the congregation. This is quite common. Most people gravitate toward a group for a sense of belonging.

I did not realize until much later that much of the searching by my parents, shared by my brother and I, was built up guilt stemming from their upbringing and their parents. Specifically, my father had conflicts with Catholicism stemming from his school days. He went to a Catholic school up through middle school. Finally after having multiple run-ins with the nuns over conflicts in conformity and reasoning, he was "encouraged" to explore other institutions of education, nun style. It appears that the proverbial "apple" did not fall far from the tree.

For me, cracks of conflict began subtly appearing early on in childhood. For example, while attending a church youth camp bible study, or "Jesus in a bus" as we called it, we were taught that only humans saved by Christ have souls. Thus, only humans go to heaven and therefore have God given "dominion" or control over all other creatures and nature. The modern use of the word Dominion is often mistranslated from its original meaning of stewardship. Unfortunately or fortunately for me at the time, I had a healthy awe, fascination and respect for nature from living in the foothills of the

Sierra Nevada Mountains. Therefore, I began to question the teacher and argue the point that it didn't make sense for only "us" to go off to heaven and all other beings to be damned to eternity, especially my dogs at the time, Minute and Brave, who were never given the option to be saved and were very good dogs mind you. The teacher tried to make the argument that animals don't have emotions or souls, so they are not part of the "Everlasting Kingdom of God". That triggered my anger and insulted my grade school intelligence. I knew from years of experience that my dogs did indeed have emotions. I spent most of my adolescent afternoons with them and could easily sense when they were sad, happy, depressed, scared or protective. Before I could argue much more, the teacher escorted me out of the "Class in a bus" to "cool" down and reflect on what the "real" truth was. I went to reflect alright, I ran off into the forest to "reflect" that I felt betrayed. How could God possibly be the creator of all things, including plants and animals, and leave them all out of his "everlasting kingdom"? What made humans any different from all of God's other creations? Furthermore, my best friend at the time, was Mormon, and apparently they were telling him that he was not going to be my buddy in heaven either, because I was not Mormon. I began to suspect they were wrong, and unluckily or luckily for me I was too stubborn to buy what they were selling.

Similar experiences increased my skepticism throughout the years to what I was being told, but the key point is there was a fundamental logical and emotional crisis pitting the known World, as I was actually experiencing and perceiving it, against the "Model World" I was being taught. This event triggered a reaction in me to begin questioning everything I was taught with regard to organized religion. As a child, I remember this clash of wit, will and wisdom was particularly difficult due to my learned sense of terror of disappointing "God". What I found myself thinking was, *'Instead of taking other peoples word for what "God" says, why don't I just ask him myself?'* And so I did. The "responses" I received were mostly waves of emotion and wordless thoughts instead of concrete conversational English. I was hoping for the Hollywood interpretation of God, in the form of Morgan Freeman, so we could sit and chat a spell. However, why this did not happen occurred to me much, much later.

My family lived in the foothills bordering the mountain range surrounding the Reno-Lake Tahoe area in Nevada. Anyone who has lived in a mountain town can tell you that the weather changes are so unpredictable that you might as well bring extra clothes for whatever comes that day. In September we would get fantastic changes in weather which would bring sudden and often violent thunder storms. Our home was on a hilltop, so you can imagine the dramatic closeness I felt with the clouds as the lightning strikes would appear to come down around me during thunder storms. One afternoon in a torrential sidesplitting rain, booming thunder and streaks of brilliant lightning bolts, I was at an aggressive, fateful junction in my life. It was in this circumstance, I found my young, frustrated self shouting up to the heavens, "God if I am absolutely wrong and misguided to question my church, the preachers and scriptures, tell me now, strike me down with a bolt of lightning or some other sign and I will stop." For a split second I thought I was done for, but alas, nothing happened. The rain continued as the lightning slowly distanced itself from me and I was left alone. The destructive force of a lightning bolt jolting through my soul never arrived. This may sound strange to the outside viewer, but if I had been hit or some dramatic sign been displayed as I suspect many people have asked for over the millennia, my curiosity would have been satisfied with a definitive answer. However, because there was no dramatic objection to my activities, I took that as positive proof that my questioning was within the boundaries of what "God" wanted me to do.

Now, this example was dramatic, from the viewpoint of a young child questioning authority and facing fears imposed upon me through my religious upbringing. From that critical intersection in my life, I continued absorbing any text I could get my hands on venturing that someone may yield some insight. My views and imagination began to change quickly. For instance, I was the only boy in 3rd grade do a science report on Black Holes. I also learned quickly that some ideas I had to keep to myself for fear of real or perceived retribution. For a while, I meandered back and forth between extremes, from astronomical topics such as white dwarfs and the structure of the known Universe to the obscure such as psychic abilities and past lives. By the time I was 13 years old, I had mostly tore down my original religious model of the Universe and began trying to assemble a new model from scratch based upon the Universe as I was experiencing it, not from some past perspective, knowledge-limited scripture taught to me by people who could not answer fundamental paradoxes. Yet, I was still battling the emotional consequences of having departed from the "flock". Guilt, shame and the pervasive fear, which fed them, overwhelmed me at times. However, in the darkest times, the seed of something new germinated, a profound *'sense'* that I thought was lost to me, the sense of peace. This peace and accompanying compassion seemed to spark from nowhere. What was the source of this 'sense'? I did not know at the time. I had my suspicions, but very limited knowledge and resources to draw upon.

Since my teen years, I have progressively evolved through three such reconstructions of a theory explaining the nature of existence and the Universe. Each iteration incorporated new knowledge gained over the years. I was not aware until I was an adult that there are, and have been, many others that have embarked on this path, some with similar results. To my surprise, the models that come the closest to what I propose in this book are ironically from 'hard-core' scientists with specialties such as physicists, biologists, complexity theorists and neurophysiologists with some contributions from particular philosophers, psychologists and spiritualists. This relative kinship gives me courage to continue.

Thus with all of us, there can be a sense of fear with change. For many people, even the thought of change makes them feel uncomfortable. Therefore, as you are reading this book now, I understand completely that when I ask you to open up to the possibility of change, particularly with something as profound as your belief system, I don't suggest this lightly. I fully expect that readers will have some fear and distrust at the prospect, so this next section was written for you. It is a path through the fear (by no means the only one) that you can follow. This path can be particularly helpful, if you are someone who has been rigorously taught a set of beliefs. So let's now face our fears.

FACE YOUR PROGRAMMED FEAR

As introduced in the previous chapter, we are taught some basic assumptions about our existence, our world and our faith. Let's break these down from their origins to the basic principles of wisdom which are universal for all of us. What remains is, for the most part, political, controlling and dogmatic expression, that pits us against one another. Why would any divine rule maker wish to do that? To what end? We know all life on Earth is cut from the same biological cloth (carbon and hydrogen atoms, nucleic and amino acids), why should humans be bent on destroying each other in the name of who is most righteous? Let's start examining the rules and sorting into wise and otherwise

Rule #1: Do not kill or cause harm.

This rule appears to be fairly benign to most of us. Typically there are major consequences in most societies if one kills or harms another. This is one rule that stands necessary if we are to have any semblance of civilization. However, as with all things in life, exceptions to the rules are always considered. What do you do if someone, who is not following Rule# 1, is intent on killing your child, loved one, friend or some other innocent? Is it then appropriate to kill in defense of another or yourself? All but the most passive monks would agree that this would be an appropriate use of force. So much so, that most government policies regarding the policing of their people accept this as a justified case for using the means necessary to protect the populace.

Ironically, some religions or religious controlled states apply exceptions to Rule #1 when it comes to gendercide in the form of "honour" killing. "Honour" killing is defined as an actual or "perceived" immoral behavior (21). A typical case study according to the non-profit organization, *Gendercide.org* is a brother, father or male cousin killing a female family member, who was 'dishonored' by having the audacity to *allow* herself to be raped! Even if the woman had followed every code of conduct by being chaperoned, covered in a cowl and a virgin up until her rape, the "honour" killing is justified by assuming that it was the woman or girl's fault for tempting, seducing and inviting the assault by the man. Furthermore, little to no punishment, accountability or responsibility for actions is born onto the man who performed the heinous 'dishonoring' act to begin with.

As with this case, you have to ask yourself the question, "Is true morality being taught here, or is the religion teaching immoral behavior in order to achieve some other lever of control?" A quick way to decipher this is to ask the question, who benefits and who pays? In this case, men clearly have the advantage not only physically, but also in their religious doctrine. What is to stop any man from exercising his frustration, for whatever reason, on a hapless female, and blame her after the fact? It is no wonder why many countries with strong women's rights are trying to put international pressure on countries that condone such devaluation of women.

Other issues with exceptions to Rule #1 lead us to Rule #2.

Rule #2: If you need to kill or harm, make sure they belong to some "other" group, not "ours."

This rule, derived from religious dogma, appears, at the very least, offensive, and at most, immoral. Why would anyone wish to harm or kill another just for thinking differently? In real life, Rule #2 is mostly practiced by individuals unless provoked or promoted by a larger entity (i.e. state warfare, civil war or revolution) with a few notable exceptions. Violent 'Mob Mentality', as it has been studied in psychology and ethics circles, often overrides our natural boundaries of behavior and would fall under the unorganized group category (22). Many of us have experienced milder forms of this phenomenon. Were you ever part of a crowd that was moved to an emotional fervor ranging from reverence or anger? Particular examples are rock concerts, football games or moving speeches or sermons. If you have, you are experiencing a collective amplification of emotions with the crowd (e.g. Herd or Mob Mentality) (23). The mechanisms as to how these signals propagate and amplify are not known; however, theories suggest a possible cascade effect where there are subtle interactions between people such as integrated audio-visual social cues or perhaps pheromones that amplify the overall emotion which cause participants to spiral out of their normal behavioral limits (24). In the journal *Neuroscience*, scientists Peter Kirsch and colleagues found the Oxytocin neuropeptide counteracts elevated fear and aggression in individual and collective behavior. It is believed that this neural peptide helps humans function as social creatures by allowing trust bonds to be formed, similar to other social species. Perhaps there are even more subtle interactions we are unaware of.

The point here is that when particular groups with fragile personalities are exposed to this type of experience, they become very suggestible, impressionable or more easily influenced. Meaning, they are more likely to buy what anyone is selling or behave in a manner that they individually would not. That suggestion could be as innocuous as supporting the home team against the visitors. The suggestion could be somewhat offensive by telling everyone break out their drugs and be free, or to downright deplorable by telling a congregation of fervent worshipers that "others" outside the chosen group are sinners or "cockroaches" and need to be eliminated. Here in the United States, most moderate Christians, Jewish, Buddhists, Hindu's, and Islamists think that is a bit of an extreme example. But that exact atrocity has happened in Rwanda between two Christian Catholic sects separating the Tutsis and the Hutu resulting in mass murder of an estimated 800,000 people. In fact the atrocity was far worse than the number of people slaughtered, mostly Tutsis. The Hutu militia, who carried out most of the murders, was also recruiting and corrupting children as young as 8 years old to do the killing. Many new recruits had to watch or participate in the killing of their own family as initiation into the militia, slated to become the next generation of fighters (25). How can such a massacre be accepted in the light that we are all human beings? To this day, the Roman Catholic Church, who supposedly all of these people were of the "flock", never condemned the genocide.

Ultimately, if your spirituality is controlled by external forces rather than internal balance, your beliefs are easily manipulated by those forces. If you cannot spiritually and logically stand on your own two feet in this Universe without the need for outside religious permission to do so, there should be a bright red flag in your consciousness. You should take a long hard look at whom or what is benefiting by requiring *intermediary permission* for your personal spiritual growth. I realize this feels like dangerous statement to many people, but it is intended to encourage you to think outside the box and point you in the direction of personal discovery that no one, outside of you, need be required.

Rule #3: We are good and they are different. (A.k.a. Bad)

Rule #3 is often times a precursor for Rule #2. The simplest examples are where some religions refer to practitioners of other religions as one or more of the following; heathens, sinners, infidels, unclean, unsaved, impure, dirty or even damned. Ironically, if you reflect on these terms of condemnation you may notice that you, along with the rest of us, fall into several of these classifications depending upon the subjective viewpoint. This Rule unfortunately sows the seeds of intolerance, prejudice and at worst hatred.

This bigotry of others is by no means limited to religions. We have seen throughout history and today that political parties, governments and nations frequently step into this quagmire. In the United States alone our main political parties fight like children over nuances in who is on the "right side" of the people. Furthermore, the GOP *far right* virtually self classify themselves as the "right side of righteous people", where as the Democratic *far left* are representing themselves as "for all common people". When an objective outsider examines both arguments, evidence shows that neither is correct. These party choices are limiting options to a false assumption. The false assumption is that the general populace of America is categorized by one of these two political affiliations. I argue that most people in America don't fall under such specific categories. Furthermore, it is offensive and irresponsible to marginalize people with such limited definitions. "Liberals" have just as many religious, spiritual or morally admirable people as the "religious right". Media personalities, who suggest otherwise are ignorant, hypocritical or have an agenda. For some Democrats to think they have exclusivity on sophisticated, critical, scientific thinking people are again completely misguided.

The above is one of the least offensive examples illustrating intolerance. As intolerance leads down an icy slope toward hatred, the potential for violent extremes, such as 911, the Spanish Inquisition, and the Christian Crusades, increases. Countless historical and critical texts have been written on these points, so I will not go into more detail here (26; 27).

Rule #4: Those who came before us know what is best for us.

At a glance, Rule #4 appears to have both truth and untruth. Easy cases for this rule are often found by looking within our own families and elders. I can still clearly remember my grandfather on my mother's side delivering frank but blunt advice about someone I was dating at the time. I had been waffling on whether or not I could see falling in love with this person. After perhaps five minutes of discussion with my Grandfather, he cut to the chase, "Do you love her or not?" Before I even began explaining my 'complicated' emotions he quickly interrupted me out of frustration and got up to walk out of the room. Before leaving he turned and said impatiently, "You know when you love someone. It is not something you gradually figure out, you either do...or you don't! Shit or get off the pot!" I was speechless.

Initially, I was shocked that such words would come from my, avidly church going, mild mannered grandfather. Secondly, I must have argued the point with my grandfather for months about this idea until we just stopped talking about it. Being of two very different generations with respect to dating, my grandfather and I did not see eye to eye. It was not until much later that I recognized that my grandfather also was coming from a place of love where all he wanted was to see his grandson happy.

I was 24 and dating a wonderful girl at the time. However, I could not pinpoint why I could not take the next step. Something deep within my sense of self, my soul if you will, was screaming at me to wait. We had been dating for some time and it was coming time to make a critical decision to move forward with our relationship or call it off. Eventually, we did call it off, much to my grandparents' disappointment. During this time both my grandmother and grandfather passed away and I felt a deep sense of regret and guilt that they were not able to see me as a married man.

Three years later when I was in my graduate studies, I had just about given up on finding the "one", and had resolved to focus on my research in biomedicine and consider pursuing a career in regenerative tissue engineering. I was attending Arizona State University at the time and lived in Tempe, AZ. After taking my dogs for a run on South Mountain, I found an out of the way coffee shop where I could get my dogs and I some water and a snack. It was there I met the most unusually mesmerizing person, purely by accident. Well...in truth, I was on my way to the restroom to prevent an impending accident, when I laid eyes on her. After coming up with the ever smooth line of, "Hi..." we sat and talked for almost an hour before my seals were going to literally, burst. I excused myself briefly, and unknown to me at the time, she had just made a covenant with her roommate that she was not going to give her number out to any men anymore due to a previous bad experience of a previous interest letting the air out of her tires. Ironically, the reason for her being at this exact coffee shop was to repair her tires that this person deflated. I would like to believe that this was no coincidence, but if it was, many causal events in our existence up to that point serendipitously played out in such a way for us to meet in such an unusual location outside of our normal routine.

Before we got involved, we put all of our cards on the table, played no games and vowed to be honest. Within three months of courting, we both *knew* we were falling in love. Not even a question. Once we passed our fears, built up from previous failed relationships, we gave into our feelings and never looked back. She is my one and only and I hers. To this day I still tell my wife, "You are, what I never knew I always wanted!" Turns out, I was wrong about this fascinating experience we call love and my grandfather was right. When you know, you know.

Now even with such personal evidence, do I extrapolate that everything my ancestors suggest is correct? Ironically, absolutely not! If anything, science has taught us over the years that one case study does not a law make. Our ancestors were wrong about plenty of things in the past. If that were not the case we would not have trains, cars, clean water, solar energy, bountiful food crops, medical breakthroughs, preventative polio vaccines, space exploration, science, modern dance, snowboarding, music, art and engineering.

What should be gleaned from the past is the wisdom of the cost vs. benefit of all of our progress. A few gold nuggets from our ancestors are the following statements.

- More is not always better.
- Time is more precious than money (at present we cannot make any more of it).
- Tread gently on this Earth, lest it tread upon us.

Rule #5: Do not steal or covet what others have.

This, as a rule, is followed by most individuals and completely ignored by many large entities. What do I mean? In most countries where laws are abided by, stealing is seen as universally wrong and is punishable by law. This can range from light jail time in Western countries to having a limb cut off in select Middle Eastern countries.

The idea of Rule #5 is acceptable to most of us, since there would seem to be a natural progression to corruption and societal decay if everyone were free to take what they wanted from one another. Indeed this appears to be true in developing countries where, 'he who has the most power gets to make law.' In these cases, Rule #5 is one of the first to be violated by the very powers that are enforcing the 'laws'. States begin stealing from the people. They take their land, their companies, their wealth, in the worst cases their lives. But they can never take their heart, their mind or their spirit. China illustrates a country that, according to the Wall Street Journal, has repeatedly partnered with foreign companies for manufacturing a technology, taken the partners technology, reverse-engineered it and created state sponsored companies that duplicate the same technology. Such actions violate their partner's international intellectual property rights and oftentimes China claims the technology as its own. China's state supported companies then push out the competition and the selective 'acquisition' of intellectual property and knowhow is complete. This practice is still a raging debate within political circles at the World Trade Organization (WTO) and is still a foreign relations sticking point particularly between the US and China (28).

It is apparent then, that in order for this rule to work, <u>everyone</u> needs to follow it, especially those in power. Therefore, laws that protect the meek and the masses from those in power are necessary to prevent thievery. When those in power chronically violate this rule, revolutions, war and potential genocide may break out. Therefore, the ideal of Rule #5 is meritorious, but requires all players, whether they are countries, corporations or citizens to play by this enforceable rule.

Rule #6: 'We' are right and 'They' are ignorant of the truth (a.k.a. wrong)

In the root of Rule #6 we have another 'us' versus 'them' scenario. This brings up two fundamental questions. Who are we? Who are they? If 'we' are fundamental Christians, then 'they' may be fundamental Islamists and vice versa. However, if 'we' are scientists then 'they' may be religious people. If 'we' are the workers union then 'they' must be the corporate executives. Or if "we" are political party X then "They" are political party Y.

It appears that Rule #6 mostly depends upon what groups you are associated with. Regardless of the circumstance, the fundamental point of Rule #6 pits particular groups against each other. With such ambiguity how are we supposed to understand the true meaning from this rule? Do we keep it or do we need to toss the rule all together?

To get a relative perspective on the situation let's humor a scientific concept called Force. Newton's 3rd Law states, "For every action there is an equal and opposite reaction." Applied to human conflict, if "we" act in a way that tries to pull or "Force" others to our viewpoint, an equal opposition reaction "Force" is pulling on "us". Ironically, when polar views give up trying to "Force" others to agree with them, the tension disappears. Therefore, it seems that if we all recognize that our species is relatively young when compared to the Universe, we all, in fact, know very little. Since our lack of knowledge of the infinite is far greater than our knowledge, it is simply arrogant, irresponsible and arguably immoral for any of us to pronounce that we are right and all others are wrong. The best we can do is to follow our nature to investigate and explore. We need to keep learning and comparing our past assumptions with new discoveries. Finally, we should always be open, aware and present to the future. From one of his famous lectures, the late Nobel Prize winning Physicist, Richard Feynman concluded with, "...ultimately the only thing we know, is that we are wrong."

Rule #7: The Divine Source, (Allah, Brahman, Bhagwan, God, Jehovah, Shangdi, Waheguru, Yahweh or other favored deity), favors us over them.

No other rule has probably caused more conflict, war and suffering than this one. Before we dive too deeply into the reasoning of Rule #7, let's guide the conversation with some ground rules. Most of the readers may have heard a few of the names listed above, but history reveals hundreds more. Since any name that humans use to describe an omniscient entity is riddled with baggage and preconceived dogmatic ideas, I choose to borrow a phrase from a well know author and thinker Dr. Wayne Dyer, which seems to capture the divine essence, 'Divine Source' or 'Source'.

Competing names for the 'Divine Source', is nothing new. Over the millennia, human societies have competed for the rights to boast who has the 'best' name for the 'Divine Source'. In fact, I just did it again in this text for conceptual and clarification reasons. In the 17th century, Athanasius Kircher (1602-80), a scholar, Jesuit-priest, scientist, and perhaps one of the first Egyptologists, developed an elaborate and artful classification diagram of 72 of the many names the Divine Source at the time (See Figure 2).

Figure 2: Kircher's Conceptual Diagram of the Names of God from Oedipus Aegyptiacus Classis IV: Cabala Hebraeorum, pp 209-266 (1652-54 CE).

I must admit, there is far more dedication and diligence put forth in the design and detail of the diagram than most of us would effort today. However, even with the beauty and complexity of Kircher's diagram, it still is, at its core, a list of names, nothing more, and nothing less. Yet this simple idea of the 'right' or more correctly 'righteous' name has been the source of terrible atrocity at the hands of man over the ages.

Some say it is the instinctual human desire to be right that leads to such atrocity. Personally, I typically reserve that need to be "right" for my wife at home. I am wise enough to realize that sometimes even when you win, you lose. We should all pick our battles carefully.

Historical atrocities in the name of, <insert your chosen deity name here>, had more to do with who thought they were more righteous. Ironically, synonyms for righteous are "blameless" or "untarnished" which I find fascinating, since even according to New Testament Christian scripture, Jesus says "let anyone among you who is without sin be the first to throw a stone..."John 8:7. Although the writings of "John" take place perhaps up to 200 years after the death of Jesus, thus little evidence that this is a true testament of what Jesus said; the wisdom of the statement is profound.

Ironically, many conservative evangelistic Christians are ready, bound and determined to judge others on how badly they are sinning. Some emanate a self-righteous, 'we know what's good for you' attitude and in extreme cases fight you to prove the point. Perhaps if they heeded their own scripture better they would not feel the need to push their way of thinking on others. Most modern day Christians would be shocked to learn that roots of religious terrorism were historically invented by early Christian Maccabees against the pagan king of Syria later followed by the Zealots against Rome's pagan emperor. These early Christians embraced martyrdom in the name of Yahweh (2).

Let me clarify. This is by no means just an evangelistic or fundamentalist Christian trait. Many fundamentalist or extreme groups of many religions share this egoistic trait. The Taliban in Afghanistan are a religiously and politically motivated fundamentalist Islamic group bent on the same end, but from a different culture of faith.

Fortunately, most of the human race is not as radical nor is as quick to judge others. However, we of the more middle ground need to be extra vigilant and careful to protect the rights of others views, while expanding our collective perception and notion of Spirituality in the context of our Universe.

Probably our greatest priority if we are to survive as a species is to advance our understanding of the Universe in which we live and how humankind and all life integrates with it. If we don't succeed in this endeavor, the loudest and most extreme minorities will control the majority and humanity may be destined to doom itself in a mass herd effect toward destruction.

In summary, it does not make logical sense that an omnipotent Source would require or prefer one restrictive human name over another. Why? For what purpose does the Source need or care for a particular name? Perhaps, instead, it matters more the context in which the name is used. Is the human chosen name used to create beauty, or is the name warped into a battle cry for destruction?

Try the following thought exercise:

1. What would the Source desire for ALL life not just humans?"
2. From a universal viewpoint, what would this same being NOT want to have happen?
3. Repeat steps 1 and 2 several times continually adapting your answers with what you learn.
4. Write down your thoughts

The first time you perform this exercise find a quiet place isolated from external stressors and interruptions. Try at first closing your eyes while taking slow, deep breaths to help relax and focus the mind. As you get better at this, incrementally increase the time according to what your schedule allows. You may want to keep a journal of your thoughts and feelings as they come to light. Understand that with repeated practice, what you may find does not always stay constant. Also, don't be surprised if what you find varies with other peoples' attempts to answer the same questions.

> **Rule #8: 'Our' holy writings are holier; and therefore, a more accurate truth than everyone else's.**

Notice that Rule #8 is a subtle justification for Rule #7. Holy writings and scripture are the bread and butter defense for most religious zealots. Conflicts and arguments that arise from Rule #7 usually boil back to Rule #8 as to who has the true writings that reflect the Divine Source's wishes. The writings also act as the source for rules and punishments for those who don't obey, although most religions have modified the code of conduct according to various interpretations or to just suit their needs. *All* organized religions have fallen or are falling into this self entrapped way of thinking. This is not to say that all religions cannot adapt and dig themselves out of a hole of interpretation, but this usually has happened with the aid of outside influences such as scientific discovery, natural consequences, conflicting experiential evidence and uprisings. Even then, significant changes in thinking that deviate from the literal readings of these "scriptures" require human kind's most noble attributes such as: courage, imagination, scrutiny, bravery and intelligence. All too often, as in the case of Galileo's publication of the *Sidereus Nuncius* in March of 1610 on Heliocentrism, personal sacrifice was required to seek out wisdom vs. dated ideals. To learn more I suggest reading Albert Van Helden's English translation called *Sidereus Nuncius, or The Sidereal Messenger* (29).

Before college, I had thought that most religious scholars were finding circular arguments to prove what they wanted to believe rather than what answers nature provided. Surprisingly, many religious scholars don't fall into the category of blind belief in what was written in spiritual texts and thus violate Rule #8. This revelation was quite astonishing to me. When I was a young man studying Engineering at University of Texas at Austin, I took a World Literature course taught by a religious scholar, ancient languages expert and former priest. Through the course of our studies we examined several examples of both blind teachings and challenges to these teachings.

For example, many religious scholars, such as Bishop Virgilius of Salzburg (c. 720-784), Hildegard of Bingen (1098-1179), and Thomas Aquinas (c. 1224-74) in the Roman Catholic Church, all before the time of Christopher Columbus, believed and taught of a spherical world, not flat. Thus the church did not see a problem with Columbus's idea to sailing to India via a western route, what they questioned was the size of the world which they believed was much larger than Columbus had anticipated.

Sadly, this history is not what is taught to children growing up in the United States. When I was a child and even today this myth is still propagated. I was taught that the Spanish Roman Catholic Church, who commonly consulted with the Spanish royalty, shunned the idea of Columbus's proposed trip. Had this been the case, why did King Ferdinand and Queen Isabella, seem to *not* listen and chose to fund the expedition anyway (30)? In reality, Queen Isabella desired to spread Christianity to the "unsaved" Indians and saw Columbus's quest as a stepping stone toward that end (along with the promises of rich rewards). Prior to the Spanish royal sponsorship, King John II of Portugal did not turn Columbus down for believing the world was flat, he knew it was round. King John II refused because he thought the world much larger than Columbus calculated, similar to the Roman Catholic scholars, and was actually correct (31).

To further examine Rule #8 we need to define a 'scripture' or holy writing. What separates a scripture from any other religious writing? Why certain writings are designated as more holy or truthful than others? Who decides? If you wish to be really bold, next time you are around a figure of "authority" in an organized religion, politely ask them the questions above. See what happens. Do not get offended and if this individual answers, listen carefully. The politely thank them for their clarification and walk away. Doing this a few times and you will get some interesting patterns of answers in four typical forms:

1. "The writings are directly written or spoken as the 'Word' by God, Allah, Jehovah, or other deity"
2. "The writings are inspired by God, Allah, Jehovah or other deity."
3. "The writings were the spoken word of Jesus, Mohammad, Moses, Joseph Smith, Bahá'u'lláh, Zoroaster, Budda, or other holy human."
4. "The writing(s) are part of the holy (Bible, Qur'an, I Ching, Torah, Dao De Jing, Kabbalah or other holy scripture.)"

The first statement assumes that the Divine directly wrote or spoke the words and some lucky lottery winner was there to take notes. It also assumes that the Divine Source desires to communicate with humans in the form of the written word limited by the languages of that time. So why only write ~2000 years ago, not prior and not now? Why do we humans have to keep imperfectly translating from ancient mostly unused, languages to commonly used ones now instead of the Source sending an updated, version 2.0 if you will. Humor aside, we actually have no proof of the Source directly writing anything since all writings that have been mentioned had the hand of humankind putting ink to papyrus. This result is in direct conflict with the concept of 'divine writings' in our list. Therefore, the second response, 'divine inspiration' in our list above usually replaces the first, 'divine writings'.

I am inspired by the Divine Source to write this manuscript. What I have just written may inspire you, anger you with my arrogance or put you on the defensive. "What is this guy talking about?" Even though I may feel and think this way, is this enough for an outside observer to verify the claim as true? What is the difference between my statement above and a spiritual guru? How does it compare to David Koresh, Jesus Christ, Joseph Smith or Mohammad? Depending upon your religious and spiritual upbringing, you will come to highly varied conclusions between what is prophetic work and what is blasphemy. My point is this, just because some group or consensus says a particular writing, orator or author was inspired by the Divine Source, does not make it so.

The contrasting point of view to the above argument may be; until we can tap the connection between the human minds and 'divine' influences, how can we argue against divine inspiration. Perhaps as we explore what is known about any such connection, we can get a better answer. Therefore, 'divine inspiration', 'divine word' or 'divine by association' are not solid arguments to make a distinction between Holy Scripture versus individual Holy Experience. Therefore, we cannot, with any amount of certainty, claim that anything written by man is any holier than any other 'scripture'.

What many of these writings *do* seem to categorically contain is 'Wisdom for living', even if imperfect. Upon studying many of these works, one begins to notice the lessons of life that ring true to most people. It is these golden pieces of wisdom that allow us to see into ourselves, to our very Nature, and thus become inspired to study further. Notice, I said "Wisdom for living". The living component is key, since it puts our responsibility in the present during our life, not in some obscurely referenced afterlife of which there are as many variations as there are colors in a rainbow.

Rule #9: Spread our Word to others and give donations to us since we know what is best.

While examining Rule #9, refer back to my earlier statement that once an entity establishes existence; it acts to perpetuate that existence. All organized religions, corporations, governments, ant colonies, cities, bacteria, humans, viruses follow this principle. There are examples, such as mortal injury, debilitating legal action or flooding, where conditions change to prevent continued existence, but this is usually due to some outside force and influence. Therefore, Rule #9 has a direct relationship with and reinforces that principle. As with all complex interactive systems that occur in nature and in life, we should expect institutions to want to continue. People that make up an institution depend upon those institutions for survival. I may not like the actions of a particular company, but that same company may be providing for thousands of families to survive. Very similarly, the human body is built for survival. Your individual cells absolutely depend upon the food you eat, the air you breathe and the water you drink. Which one of us would want to choose to waste away or destroy ourselves without some good reason? Religious institutions are no different. They strive to survive and grow.

This is a fundamental principle in Nature for any universal complex adaptive systems and should be expected. Does that fundamental principle mean that the second part of the rule #9 is true, that 'we know what is best'? Do all institutions know best? If that were true, then we have an undefined definition of what is 'best'. Most institutions 'think' they know what they are doing; however, if you survey the people that they affect, you will probably get close to a split decision. More correctly, an institution or entity will try to do what is 'best' for itself.

Rule #10: Do NOT question the Rules even if they conflict with observation!

It is safe to say that if you have read this far you have already violated Rule #10 by questioning the previous rules. Congratulations! You are starting to discriminate between wisdom, dogma and manipulation. Being open to possibility and having the courage to honestly analyze historical information is the first step to understanding spiritual and scientific information. Our very existence is simultaneously an exhilarating epiphany and a terrifying precipice near the vast chasm of unknowns. I call this the chasm of doubt and fear.

Insight #1: "Leap, the chasm is illusion."

One of the most difficult and fearful times, particularly for those of us who have been indoctrinated to think in particular ways, is navigating through the 'breakdown' that follows from letting go of preconceived notions about existence. Therefore, I will share insights throughout the book, like the one above, from my personal experiences. However, understand that all experiences are colored through the observer's perspective. Thus you will perceive insights slightly differently than me or anyone else. Armed with this knowledge, let's face the chasm of opportunity and walk through the breakdown together.

CHAPTER 3
BREAKDOWN

-All things operate in cycles, life is no different-

ANCHORLESS

As we take the leap into the unknown our safety nets, preconceived notions, dogma and the rest of our personal house of cards fail us. When this event occurs, don't despair. Instead, begin to find the 'Flow'. This sounds like a stock answer at first, but it is a fundamental step toward open thought. Perhaps a grandparent, parent or friend has relayed similar sagely advice as, "Go with the flow!" There is substantial wisdom with this notion even if only said in jest or to ease pain.

At this stage of personal exploration, most people want to take the reins and control their destiny. What is often found is the more you try to force a situation, the larger the fight or obstacle appears. Since the dawn of Newtonian Mechanics, science has long known that a force applied gives rise to an equal and opposite resisting force. When people face resistance, particularly with their own spiritual growth, the typical behavior is to constantly increase effort, which ironically seems to achieve smaller and smaller improvements in the direction of your life. The more you fight, the tougher life seems to push back. The long term side effects to this approach are fatigue, frustration and doubt. With this uncertainty, most people 'about face' and return to their dogmatic belief system, because it seems easier in the short term.

The danger of taking the easy route is you end right back where you started, with the same questions, the same disappointments and same disillusions. Unfortunately, many people yearning to stretch their spiritual and intellectual wings get psychologically battered into submission by their reemergence of fear and doubt. This chapter may perhaps be the most important, for if you cannot pass the chasm of doubt and despair, you will only move alongside the precipice of indecision. The last thing you want to do at this point is to get lost in the fog and circle back to where you started.

How do you overcome the doubt and despair chasm? The simple answer is you don't. Now that may sound like a copout but let's examine the word overcome in more detail. The idea to 'overcome' something is by the Webster's Dictionary definition *to gain superiority, conquer, defeat, or prevail over a thing, obstacle or situation.* If the obstacle is doubt and fear, they will both with equal magnitude and in opposition to your efforts. Then you are at an eternal impasse. Therefore, what use is it to keep performing the same action and expect different results? Therefore, sometimes the best action is *non-action.* As previously stated, more force simultaneously increases resistance, so what happens when you don't provide any force? As you may suspect, 'nothing' or 'no-thing' happens. The obstacle simply ceases to resist you.

To illustrate this example more concretely, let's go back to the mental picture of the precipice of indecision looking over the chasm of doubt and despair. Unconsciously, most people use their childhood understanding of spirituality (their religious teachings) to keep them 'grounded'. They are literally 'anchored' to the precipice by rules and dogma conceived by some invisible implied authority. Although, this 'anchor' feels like a form of security keeping the individual from falling into the chasm, in reality it is a terrible burden, constraining the individual. So much so, that they cannot hope to cross the chasm of doubt let alone launch toward their full potential. Moreover, their mind and body (in the form of pathology) are bound to drag this anchor around with them until they become bitter and disenchanted with life, effectively prohibiting their innate ability to evolve as a spiritual and vibrant being. When the individual finally gets the courage to try to cross the chasm, he or she will typically pull on the chain that shackles them to the anchor. Low and behold the anchor pulls back just as hard. So you see, you can pull and drag your anchor of closed mindedness and limited thinking, but in the end you will still be dragging your own resistive force to meaningful change with you.

So if more force is not the answer, how do you free yourself with this anchor constantly tugging at you? The answer is simple, yet MOST people cannot come to terms with this simple idea shown in Insight #2.

Insight #2: Let go of what you know

You mean I cannot take my baggage or previous knowledge (anchor) with me? NO! Your baggage is the past, leave it there and ignore it for the time being and live in the present. NOW is the only real moment in which you can affect change. It is the final act of cutting the chain that keeps you tied to your anchor. The anchor represents your preconceived ideas of how everything in the Universe works; your story of you, everyone and everything around you. You may be the wisest person on the planet or haven't thought much beyond your next meal. Either way, you must let go of these limitations in order to begin anew. An old Zen teaching describes a wise Japanese Zen master (disputed to be Nan'in, but origins are unclear) (32). The Zen koan (story) is as follows from a translation by Paul Reps called *Zen Flesh, Zen Bones*:

> Nan'in gave audience to a visiting professor of philosophy,
> Serving tea, Nan-in filled his visitor's cup, and kept pouring.
>
> The professor watched the overflow until he
> could restrain himself no longer:
>
> "Stop! The cup is overfull, no more will go in."
>
> Nan-in said,
>
> "Like this cup, you are full of your own opinions and speculations.
>
> How can I show you Zen unless you first empty your cup?"

Letting go of needing to impose or "force" your preconceived ideas on to the surrounding world, relieves the tension in the tether which is anchoring you to a particular way of thought. Ignore the obstacles, which appear to lie before you, and focus on a solution. See your place in that solution, and almost effortlessly, the obstacle may have moved, became small, or disappeared all together. Notice that you "feel" lighter, almost weightless. Your mind is more nimble and childlike again, with a greater sense of possibility. This does not mean that you will never encounter further obstacles, but it does suggest a way for you to navigate to solutions despite the rise and fall of such obstacles. This concept is just as important with everyday life experiences as it is with spiritual independence and enlightenment.

WHY?

The most common questions or statements I get when I tell people Insight #2 is "Why?"

- "Why do I need to let go of what I know?"
- "Why should I? I have gained a lot of knowledge in my life; I am not just going to throw all my knowledge away just because someone tells me too."
- "I am comfortable with my beliefs; I don't need to change."
- "How dare you tell me that the <insert holy text here> is wrong?
- "I am already well versed in the sciences and history and have no need to redefine my existence. Why should I?"

The answer is already lying just below the surface of these questions. The resistance to letting go is a product of the uncertainty and emotions clinging to what you know or think you know. Now does that mean that we throw the proverbial "baby out with the bathwater?" For now, yes! Ultimately we will find our way forward and integrate what we have learned from our travels, but for now we need a clean slate and ONLY a clean slate from with which to start. For if a picture is already cluttering the canvas of our mind, how can we possibly create and discover something truly novel?

THE COLOR OF UNCERTAINTY

Here is an interesting mental exercise. Please try to perform the exercise before reading on, so as to not have any preconditioned notion of an answer. Again find a quiet place for an uninterrupted time of between 5-15 minutes. Sit calmly and imagine, if you will, a void or empty space. Hold that thought and transform it into an image in your mind. Afterwards, record what you see?

This exercise can tell you a bit about yourself and how you view emptiness. When I perform surveys with my students, most will have an image of pure blackness "the abyss", the empty vastness of space or sometimes an empty white space.

Some psychologists think that colors are related to human's sense of meaning and belief. Throughout time, the psychology of the color black has changed. In fact many cultures view black differently. In the US "westernized" culture, subconscious meanings of black is often associated with evil, malevolence or death. In "eastern" cultures the "black-belt" in martial arts represents power and control. Ironically, although black has an ominous feeling about it for many modern westerners, ancient Egyptian's identify black with "life and rebirth". Therefore it is nearly impossible for there to be a universal "meaning" of a color other than the scientific quantification of wavelength or frequency associated with the various colors of the spectrum. Cultural, psychological and temporal influences affect what one interprets as the "meaning" of a color (33).

Ask yourself the question, "what does the color "mean" or "feel" like to me?" What emotions or associations does concentrating on the color evoke? Warmth? Strength? Power? Newness? Evil? Doubt? Fear? Loneliness? Despair? If you are like the majority of westerners, you probably experience some emotion similar or related to the latter five. If you have other positive thoughts and/or thought of another color to begin with, congratulations. You have probably confronted some spiritual or psychological doubts in your life and overcome some of them before. The purpose of this exercise was to get you to realize one salient point:

Insight #3: Your doubts and fears are ONLY emotional responses arising from the feeling of powerlessness, nothing more.

As such, doubts, fears, feelings of uncertainty are all subjective emotional experiences that are just as much a product of your culture and upbringing as they are your life experiences and confusion. With this knowledge, learn to recognize such emotions and impulses. Let them pass through you and when they diminish, you will remain. You will still have your faculties about you. With practice, your confidence in accepting fear and channeling that energy instead of buckling under it, will increase. Eventually, you will become empowered knowing that fears, doubts and uncertainties that have been directing your life for so long are insignificant hiccups in the course of your awakening life. No longer let these irrational emotional impulses force your thinking.

I am not presenting a new concept here; I am restating in a modern way some of the teachings of the past. The Tibetan Buddhism practice has many ways of dealing with fear, primarily by using focused breathing and visualization techniques. However, I think the teachings of Shantideva are the most practical. To paraphrase, "...if there is a frightening situation and we can do something about it, why worry, just do it. If there is nothing we can do, then why worry, it won't help..." (34)

Tibetan Buddhism recognizes a female Buddha-figure, Tara, which represents the energy-winds of body and breath. Tara is also the aspect of Buddha that protects us from fear. Thus, by metaphorically taking the leap over your personal chasm of doubt and despair, symbolically take a cue from Tara and ride the fated winds. Simply, all you have to do to keep from falling into obscurity is focus on your breath (the "the energy-winds") which guide you onward.

Insight #4: When facing doubt and uncertainty, just breathe.

TRAVELING THE WINDS OF CHANGE

You are now primed to take on your continued journey toward deeper spiritual understanding. You may begin to see new possibilities now open to you from this higher vantage point. Perhaps you are asking yourself, "Which idea do I choose to investigate first? How do I know if something is actual evidence of spiritual existence in this Universe or if it is pure speculation? How do I keep from being reeled in by every charlatan fishing for uncertain minds and getting duped?"

Relax. Breathe.

For now, enjoy the journey. Feel the excitement and bliss associated with such fantastic possibilities. Travel where life takes you. A relatively safe place to begin is traveling the 'winds' of your own mind. Silent meditation works for many who practice the art. For those with more academic training, exercises in pure logic, thought experiments or inner debate are helpful tools as well. The nice thing about meditation is that you essentially focus on a thought or present experience for several slow breaths in a quiet place and then let go of the moment to then just breathe again. All the while, be aware and present in the stillness. Perhaps not the first or even third session, but eventually you receive a 'gut' answer. The answer may appear as your own thought, yet you cannot quite remember the origin. It may or may not come with language, meaning the idea may present itself as an intuition, a symbol or even in some unorthodox situations as an algorithm, vision or mathematical expression. Being a trained engineer and scientist, I have experienced all of these responses.

If you ask a scientifically trained person how they achieved some of their greatest ideas, chances are you will get one of the following answers:

- "I was (walking, hiking, showering, dreaming or other passive activity) when it hit me."
- "I had an unexpected experimental outcome (a.k.a. fortunate accidental result)."

Sometimes, focused logical thought will generate these answers, which usually requires one to mitigate emotional and bias attachments to the outcome. This method is difficult for many people without proper training, and thus is typically only used by professional philosophers, theoretical physicists, scientists, mathematicians and the like.

You may be questioning, "Wait a minute, you are telling me that professional philosophers meditate?" In a manner of speaking, yes.

The American Heritage Dictionary defines the verb *meditate* as "to reflect on, contemplate". The Buddhism and Hinduism definition for *meditate* is, "to train, calm or empty the mind, often by achieving an altered state, as by focusing on a single object." If we expand the definition to include European etymology, we define *meditate* as, "to engage in devotional contemplation, especially prayer." Finally, a more modern interpretation yields, "To think or reflect, especially in a calm and deliberate manner." So you see, the term meditate is essentially a deep state of concentration and contemplation. Whether that state is focused on breathing and stillness in line with Eastern traditions or a deep state of focused concentration and contemplation of a question in Western academic thought, the results are very similar. At some point a plausible answer bubbles to the surface of the meditators consciousness. How this happens is still a mystery.

Most of us, regardless if we are scientists, mathematicians, artists, engineers, psychologists, physicists or other highly cerebral professions, have an epiphany during relaxing states between sessions of mental exertion. Think back to a significant problem you had when you were young. You may have continuously stressed, thought about the problem and worried incessantly about how to solve it while the answer eluded you for perhaps hours or days. More often than not, an answer came to you when you least expected it. Sometimes the solution emerged in your sleep. Other times it appeared first thing when you awoke or while bathing or jogging. Unless we previously knew the answer, the solution rarely comes to us at the exact time of our choosing.

The only difference between you and great thinkers of history, such as, Albert Einstein, Max Planck, James Maxwell, Sir Isaac Newton, Charles Darwin, Nichola Tesla, Immanuel Kant, Aristotle and Plato, is they were highly trained in their areas of expertise. Greatly benefitting from information learned on paths not to take, they meditated on a specific problem deeper and longer than others. Their persistent focus led them toward historic revelations. Here lies the realm of creative thought. Modern scientific and theoretical inquiry uses these same principles; thus, scientists and thinkers are the philosophers of modern day. Their minds flow with the winds of change and meditate to discover where they lead. Now that you have opened up your mind to possibilities outside of your past, so can you.

CHAPTER 4
RESURRECTION

For though she burnest blighted breath
So fiercely brilliant unto death
Tumbling dust from up on high
Invisible to mine naked eye
Down in ashen bed she lay
Through night I wait in my dismay
Till Dawn spreads its morning light
New life longs for virgin flight

FINDING YOUR INSPIRATION

Now that you know *how* to travel the winds of change via open minded meditation, you may find yourself in the precarious position of defining *who* you now are. Where do you fit into this new paradigm? Think of this as a metaphorical resurrection into a new way of being. The world looks, feels and *is* different to you from here on out.

As you may have already noticed, your perception of reality is perhaps different from when you began this book. From the ashes of your former blind, anchored and isolated self, you have reemerged and begun to see new realms of possibility. I have come to call this *mental resurrection* or *the Phoenix phase*. This phase sheds the baggage that burdens your intellectual and spiritual development, enabling your mind to consider fresh ideas.

Once we pass fear, doubt and anxiety, it does not take long for something new to fill the void, a calling. A calling to explore, learn, study, meditate or create. Through it, we find the desire to expand our consciousness becomes as fundamental and integral to our human spirit as breathing. It is simply described as *hope*.

Hope may sound like an overused statement, but this is the most concise term I can find to describe the passion or inspiration that drives humanity to continue. Why do we as a species keep striving for something better? When confronted with past and present atrocities of governments, religions, corporations and peoples, why should we have any notion of better days ahead? Hope. Hope for us. Hope for our children, grandchildren and their children. Hope for all sentient life and the planet not only persists but flourishes. Hope there is something more to this existence than a lotta' YottaBytes of information and facts[2]. Hope that the seemingly endless cycles of creation, existence and destruction is progressing somewhere toward a purpose.

Whatever idea for the future motivates us; we begin leading an inspired life knowing that we are working to realizing that hope. For example, you may want to help understand the connection of genetics and generational knowledge integration. Perhaps you wish to create new models connecting humanity to the life cycles of other species, such as sea turtles. Your hope may be simpler. Perhaps you wish to find a personal connection with the divine that you can share with your children, void of traditional religious biases. Maybe, you want to contribute your skills to others in need.

Pay close attention to hope rather than fear. Hope guides you toward your passions, whereas, fear leads you astray. Talk with anyone who has lived for a considerable length of time and who you feel has had a fulfilling life. Ask them whether you should follow your passions or be conservative. I have found that most people who followed their passions are more fulfilled, happier and inspired with life. As a side benefit, these same groups of people are typically more successful and wealthy. You may view that last statement as materialistic. However, the context in which I am writing includes a broader definition of success and wealth. In this broader context, successful people feel accomplished in whatever discipline they choose regardless of specific compensation. Success

---

Yotta is the prefix for 10^{24} bytes.

becomes a fulfillment of one's purpose not a dollar amount. Wealth is then the overall feeling of abundance, purpose of mind and of soul.

A great example of monetary wealth not equating to soulful wealth is revealed in the book, *The Big Short*, by Michael Lewis. Lewis skillfully reveals the tale of many hedge fund founders and managers who created massive monetary gains for themselves and their clients during this last great recession of 2007 through 2010. However, many felt unappreciated, alone and anxious for the world. A few hedge fund managers suffered from anxiety and cardiovascular related disease as a result. Why were these people, who were successful and wealthy, according to the mantra of westernized capitalism, miserable and suffering from stress related disease? All were missing the larger component. They were *spiritually and socially void* in these pursuits, which left them longing for something different and more meaningful (35). People in my life, who I am privileged to call friends, have successfully dodged the amoral Wall Street gauntlet. They have come out of that cut throat environment literally and spiritually starving for purpose, passion and inspiration. Noble characteristics I can personally attest to are a desire to atone and a longing to contribute to the societal soul rather than taking from it.

Similarly, many wealthy founders of Dot-com companies made huge amounts of money, but the monetary wealth alone did not lead to happiness. For instance, private conversations with a former employee of one such individual, whom I will not disclose out of respect for privacy, revealed the reality of their employer's situation. The employer was a cofounder of a successful software company during the early dot com boom, and enjoyed the rapid ride to financial wealth and status with an early internet company. He was still quite young when he sold off his stake in the company and effectively 'made it' according to pure economic measures. The now multi-millionaire had more money than he would ever need in his foreseeable lifetime. One would think he was on top of the world, yet apparently he was in misery. Life no longer inspired him. He was void of purpose, which was formerly filled by the company, and sadly he spent many days alone and despondent. He lost his hope and inspiration for the future, and no amount of money would heal that. Not until a new source of hope was found in the form of personal relationships did this entrepreneur reemerge and flourish once again.

Many people in similar predicaments found ways to channel themselves toward a new hope, a new purpose in life. Before I elaborate, here is a trivia question.

What do video game founders, the Blues Brothers producer, a Landenberg Foundation executive, a Harvard MD, an executive director for the Bill and Melinda Gates foundation and a Democratic Party organizer have in common? The answer is the X-Prize Foundation shown in the network diagram in Figure 3 below:

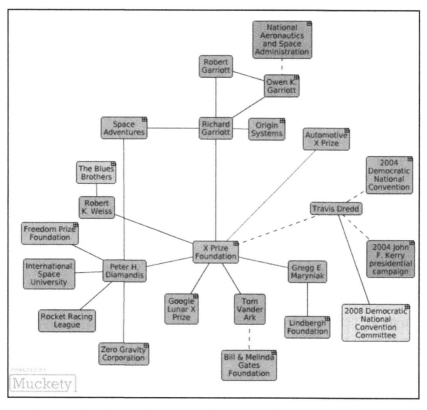

Figure 3: The X-prize Foundation Network of Visionaries' (Generated at www.muckety.com July 29th 2010)

Our tail starts with two brothers. Robert and Richard Garriott, founders of Origin games, created the early 90's hit Ultima gaming series. Upon successfully selling Origin to Electronic Arts (EA), earning them hundreds of millions, you may assume they just wanted to sit on a Tahitian beach drinking frosty beverages and tour the Asian pacific on their yachts. Not so! They reinvented themselves to create a new hope which aligned with their passions and sense of responsibility to humankind. Being sons of the former astronaut and father, Owen Garriot, they both grew up around space exploration and desperately wanted to play in that 'space'.

Around the same time, Dr. Peter Diamandis, who was MIT training in aerospace health sciences, was already involved in the Zero Gravity Corporation, a company that sells the experience of free fall to clients similar to what astronauts feel in orbit. Gregg Maryniak, the director of the Lindbergh Foundation lent the book *Spirit of St. Luis* about another visionary Charles Lindbergh to Dr. Diamandis. Peter was inspired by the story of Lindbergh and the 'Orteig Prize' idea, which spawned not only the flight of the Spirit of St. Louis, but a 300-fold increase in pilot's license applications, and about a 30-fold increase in people wanting to fly in airplanes. From his inspiration, Peter addressed the 1995 NSS International Space Development Conference with the newly sparked idea of the X-Prize concept as a way of breaking through the barriers to commercialization of low orbit space by the private sector.

Eventually the X-Prize foundation materialized in May of 1996 with financial support from Richard Garriot, and the entrepreneurial Anousheh Ansari and her brother in-law Amir Ansari. After their multi-million dollar donation, the space race X-Prize was renamed the Ansari X-Prize. Many contributing members such as Robert Weiss producer of Blues Brothers, Travis Dredd, organizer for multiple National Democratic conventions, Tom Vander Ark, representing the Bill and Melinda Gates Foundation joined. As a result the novel possibility of private commercial spacecraft emerged when Space Ship One, designed by renowned aerospace engineer, Burt Rutan with support from Microsoft co-founder Paul Allen, won the $10 million X-Prize on October 4th, 2004. The network diagram above is just a fraction of the people involved with ongoing projects at The X-Prize Foundation, which aims to make social and technical 'impossibilities', *possible*. The Foundation's collective 'Hope' is to transform space travel from limited human exploration to sustainable human existence off world.

The above story is a great example of people from all walks of life and disciplines coming together under a unified banner of hope for a brighter future. Collectively, they took the leap of faith required to brave this journey and created a new realm of *possible* from what was previously deemed impossible by 'experts.' The X-Prize story highlights one of the most powerful factors required to turn just *possible* into reality through the *power of independent thinking*.

THE POWER OF INDEPENDENT THINKING

O nce hope is allowed to flourish free from fear and doubt, then and only then can we truly begin to think freely. The ideal goal is to think unhindered by past prejudices and misconceptions. If you find that you are not close to this goal, continue working through the exercises in Chapters 1-3.

Thinking freely means being able to think outside of the confines of your previous assumptions or learned dogma. Creative people, engineers and scientist do this all the time, right? Not necessarily, most are limited by the knowledge their teachers exposed to them. It is not without considerable courage, insight and stubborn persistence that new ideas emerge and bear fruit. After all, if our ancestors believed everything their predecessors told them, the sun would still be the god RA or Apollo, the moon a goddess named Luna, the speed of sound would still be unbreakable and only wood, and ducks and witches would float on water. Well perhaps not the last one. Consider this point the next time you encounter a new idea. Before dismissing the idea as altogether rubbish ask yourself, "Is Apollo still riding his Chariot across the sky every day?"

MIND EXERCISE

A very enlightening exercise is to start questioning a personal assumption about the world around you. Try to remember, where you first learned this assumption. Who taught this assumption to you? Why did they believe it? If possible, ask that person, "Where did you learn it from?" If you cannot, try looking up the assumption in reputable sources, such as academic journals or publications. Are there some alternative ideas to your assumption? What are they and who is promoting them? How does the alternative idea compare to your original understanding? Can you create a way to test these assumptions against yours to resolve the issue?

When beginning on this process, take baby steps. Remember, if there is considerable evidence to support a theory, such as gravity, and very little evidence of an opposing theory such as, "I can fly like superman", I would caution to not perform the first experiment off of some cliff or high building! Start small. A few "up, up and aways..." on the grass might yield answers quick enough at the expense of only a skinned up a knee and perhaps a wounded ego. In admitted embarrassment, I actually did try this test when I was a child. Even when I tried adding height, via a roof, and a strong headwind, I still did not have much luck. However, I did prove that I was NOT indestructible, which is useful knowledge for a young boy of 12 to know ahead of time.

Do not succumb to pragmatism for fear of falling lest you drown your imagination in the quagmire of mediocrity. Even if your inquiry reconfirms what you have been taught, it does not mean all exploration yields the same result. There are still infinite possibilities of undiscovered intellectual country to astonish all of us by taking the path many fear to tread.

The founders of the X-Prize Foundation did not listen to 'conventional wisdom' and stop dreaming of a new reality for human space exploration. Neither should you. The founders redefined the dream, inspired the dream in others and collaborated with people with the right kinds of knowledge. Their perseverance turned the dream into possibility, and with sustained action a new reality. I call this process 'Inspired Reality Making.' Use this example as inspiration for your own life to turn dreams into reality. Transform yourself from a dreamer to a reality maker.

Insight #5: Nothing is impossible; there are only conditional impossibilities.

NEW REALMS OF POSSIBILITY

> *"Here's what I know about the realm of possibility— it is always expanding, it is never what you think it is. Everything around us was once deemed impossible. From the airplane overhead to the phones in our pockets to the choir girl putting her arm around the metalhead. As hard as it is for us to see sometimes, we all exist within the realm of possibility. Most of the limits are of our own world's devising. And yet, every day we each do so many things that were once impossible to us."*

> *— David Levithan (excerpt from The Realm of Possibility)*

There are three essential types of human behavior, with respect to spiritual thought and its relationship with manifesting possibility into reality. The three types of behavior are:

1. Makers
2. Watchers
3. Demolishers

Makers are individuals or groups that come together to create something they feel morally and often 'spiritually' compelled to do. Sometimes this motivation forms an organization to create a breakthrough event. A classic example is the formation of the National Aeronautical and Space Administration, commonly known as NASA. NASA was formed inspirationally by Makers, such as President John F. Kennedy, to launch human kind from Earth to the moon. Motivation can be simple, such as an inspired author writing a book with a compelling story or message to share. Spiritually aligned Makers not only go with the flow of the Universe but feel compelled to contribute something of worth to humanity and the world. It is an indescribable 'need' to create. For those who rarely experience this, it feels like a 'calling' to give back to the world which gives us so much.

My personal hope with the Spiritual Evolution series is to help all people find a way to their own spiritual path. I hope the path guides you to your creative 'calling', to in fact, become a Maker. Then you can participate with others like yourself to contribute at a grander scale. As I sit and write these words, to whoever reads them, I am compelled to do so. I realize that I am fortunate to have a family understanding enough, to allow me to continue this journey, where ever it leads. Of course, this assumes that my spouse's 'honey do list' is done as well.

The plural noun, Watchers, is used in this text to describe those souls who choose not to create. They choose to not commit to anything productive and become a drag on society, both physically and spiritually. The reasons for why people choose ambivalence are as varied as the colors in a Southwest sunset. The word ambivalent literally means 'unsure and of two minds'. A little uncertainty is natural and reasonable, but choosing non-participation places you in effective limbo. Organized religions seize upon this idea of limbo. However, they miss the key point. Limbo is part of living human experience here and now. Limbo is not required to describe a potential hereafter, since it is a veritable space or transition between two states. Thus, Watchers choose to watch life from the sidelines. They wait to 'see what happens' in the game of life before deciding to actually play. Unfortunately for Watchers, by the time they decide they want to contribute and play in the game of life, most of their lifetime has been spent waiting and little time is left to participate. The emotional manifestations of this predicament are regret or desperation.

Why does anyone knowingly choose to sit on the sidelines? All of us, even the most educated, active and enlightened fall into complacency for periods of time. It is our ability to recognize limbo, when we fall into it, and our ability to pick ourselves up, which separates those who walk the path from those that talk about it. Dusting ourselves off, we realign our soul and go back in for another round now as Makers.

Strikingly, many Watchers tend <u>not to be aware</u> that they are in limbo. A great analogy is dreaming while we sleep. Notice, when we dream, we rarely realize it. Similarly, Watchers navigate the directionless living dream as real, and robotically perform day to day tasks until an event 'wakes them up', and they realize that half of their life has passed them by. Fear is a strong promoter of Watcher behavior resulting in paralysis. Some people do this consciously, but most unconsciously drift into this behavior.

People's tendency for complacency is why many institutions and governments use fear as a form of citizen behavior control. Fear of failure, fear of embarrassment, fear of being judged, fear of losing everything, fear of making a mistake, the list goes on and on. We all experience these types of emotions and are empathetic to them. Emotions are particularly strong when tackling a new venture that you have never tried before. *Do not give in to these fears*, they stem from the same emotional center that create the fears we faced in Chapter 2 and have no bearing on you success.

There are ways to train yourself to recognize a dream and create it to your liking, known as lucid dreaming. I have twin 5 year old sons and an 8 year old son. I have been working with them since they were 3 to learn to modify their dreams. The short term goal is to turn nightmares into fun dreams by transforming into action heroes in their dream. My children become the hero in their own mindscape by consciously telling themselves "nothing can harm me because I make this dream and I can <insert special power here>". This simple practice allows them to vanquish their fears (monsters) and doubts (demons) and virtually save the day in the safety of their own mind. The long term goal is for them to see themselves as the maker of their dreams. If they can find the courage to be a maker in the mind, they can apply that courage in the real world, overcome adversity and open up infinite possibilities. Ultimately, my sons are learning to be living Makers.

> **Insight #6: We all have the capacity to become spiritually aligned makers. It just requires alignment, courage and sustained action.**

Other Watchers choose not to act, driven by guilt, complacency, addictions or other impairments. This category of Watcher finds it difficult to find a path out of apparent limbo having little to no spiritual alignment to guide them. Watchers suppress maker efforts by over questioning, hypercriticizing and throwing up barriers for why a new possibility is, in their mind, impossible. Even when they have positive proof, often they still shy away from this new reality. Instead Watchers continue to focus on examples that fit into their model, rather than facing the uncomfortable realization that their reality model is perhaps in need of retuning or is completely broken.

Despite these issues, Watchers do perform one vital function, maintaining the status quo. Maintenance may not sound like much, but consider situations in which change is made too rapidly and disaster results. For example, rain in proper doses sustains plants, animals and all terrestrial life. However, a torrent of rain from a hurricane or tropical storm causes flooding, damage and harm to the very lives it normally sustains. Therefore, Watchers slow dramatic changes by Makers to a more measured pace. This helps prevent catastrophic change and promotes healthy growth.

Finally, let's examine the most misunderstood type of human behavior, the demolishers. Although human kind does not like to acknowledge the existence of demolishers, except in history books, nature recognizes the balance, need and reoccurrence of the destructive role.

The drums of anger, hate, prejudice and fear combined with a sense of purpose drive demolishers. Demolishers often misplace this sense of purpose as a sense of spirituality. Interestingly, demolishers have strong passions and feel that they are Makers of a different type. This identity crisis makes it extremely difficult for demolishers to see the path they are actually on. Demolishers see many things that Makers do as an affront to their fragile reality and so they purposefully thwart Makers efforts.

Terrorism is an extreme, yet potent example of demolisher behavior. The terrorist label, in my opinion, has been greatly overused since the George W. Bush's administration's definition. Since then, many countries use the term 'terrorism' to describe almost any group that is in conflict with the governing power. My definition of a terrorist is simply, a person or entity that makes the conscious decision to kill or destroy anyone or anything (innocents, men, women, children and nature) in order to achieve his or her self-righteous goal regardless of the life cost. Others feel that there calling is to purely incite fear in their enemies. Once this choice is made, a terrorist has lost all moral and spiritual alignment with a living society and living world.

Countries, institutions and other organizations who label terrorists are not off the hook either, because they can play the demolisher role at times. When a collective organization chooses to destroy anything that threatens its existence or expansion the demolisher behavior arises. Even with the best of intentions, a deceivingly thin line separates a long term visionary group that inspires creativity and moral alignment from a short term survival institution that encourages control, status quo and profits. The later institution would rather grow itself at the expense of all else. The cellular equivalent in the human body is cancer.

In a recent example, British Petroleum (BP) (unconsciously or consciously?) slid into this role to fulfill investor growth projections. By yielding to purely economic pressures and not upholding its responsibility to the environment from which it operates and borrows oil resources, BP compromised safety mechanisms and procedures put in place that should protect against blow out failures on one of their oil wells. According to the US Department of Energy study, the result was a record total 4.9 million barrels of oil spilled into the Gulf of Mexico in 2010 overtaking the number one spot as the worst human caused environmental disaster in history. Incidentally, BP's disaster displaced the Persian Gulf War of 1991 where the dumping of oil was intentional (36). Much of the oil from the BP spill is still to this day, lying on the gulf floor measuring ~2 inches thick on top of the sediment core with unknown short and long term consequences to the once abundant see life that lives there (37).

In nature we feel large demolisher effects in the form of destructive forest fires, massive earthquakes and violent hurricanes. With our body, microscopic demolisher effects are barely noticeable in the fabric of our tissues, muscles and bones. Bones for example, heals itself by first destroying and clearing out old injured tissues and cell debris via osteoclasts (bone cells that absorb bony tissue). Osteoclasts are the demolition cells of our bones that ready an injury for reconstruction by osteoblasts (bone cells that produce bone tissues). This is a necessary function for our survival and the survival of all animals with skeletons. Therefore, demolisher behavior should not be synonymous with 'bad' behavior, but instead needs to be understood.

For thousands of years mankind has created symbols and caricatures of demolisher behavior, with a destructor or transformer theme. Hinduism has an elegant personification of the destructor, Śhiva. Śhiva is one of the "Trimurti" or one of the three personified aspects of the primal divine, Brahman. The other two faces of the Trimurti are Brahmā, the creator (Maker), and Vishnu, the maintainer (Watcher). Christianity also has its version of Śhiva in the form Christianity's destructor, Christ of the second coming, opener of the seven seals, and bringer of the four Horsemen (Revelations 6:1-8). Alternative interpretations name The Holy Spirit as the destructor equivalent of Śhiva, Christ as the equivalent of Vishnu (Krishna) and the Father as Brahmā.

These aspects of the divine parallel all three aspects of human behavior listed above. This is not by mistake; the behavioral aspects are just as valid now as they were in ancient times when man created divine personifications in his own image. I am just presenting them here without religious connotation or doctrine attached to the observation. A point to be noted here is that the three types are descriptions of human behaviors, **not entities**, as presented in ancient Hinduism. They should also not be misconstrued as *states* of being. In other words behaving like a Maker, Watcher or a Demolisher doesn't make an enlightened or unenlightened being. You may just consciously or unconsciously be fulfilling a role. Awareness of what your behavior is and why you behave in particular ways is the just the beginning to understanding. However, your conscious power to choose your behavior type is the true opening to spiritual enlightenment.

What does this all have to do with creating new possibilities? For you to create a possibility and manifest it into reality; you need to be aware of three things:

1. Your motivation,
2. Your current behavior type
3. What is your goal with this manifestation

I write this with the greatest amount of care and caution, because my goal is to help people find spiritual makers in themselves and align them with that source of spirit. Without open awareness, many people will rush to create anything, but may be driven from a passionate source of vengeance, fear or hate. They may not realize that they shifted into the destructor role.

Genghis Khan is a potent historic example of one who unintentionally slid into the destructor role. Genghis Khan was born to the Borjigin (Wolf) Tribe with the birth name Temujin, third son to Yesügei, a minor tribe Chieftain or Han. When Yesügei was poisoned by a competing tribe, Temujin was third in line to become clan Chieftain at the young age of nine. After being betrayed by his father's bondsman, Temujin's entire family was ostracized by the Wolf tribe, because the bondsman would not accept Yesügei's sons' birthright to govern. Temujin's family was left for dead, to survive on their own. These events thrust Temujin into manhood before he spiritually matured. Temujin built alliances after narrowly escaped a brief enslavement by former friendly tribes. From his adolescent traumatic experiences and need to protect the honor of his family name, Temujin eventually built an army of ~20,000 men from the wanderers of the land. Drawing from his spirit of vengeance, Temujin used his army to take back what he thought was rightfully his.

Ultimately, Temujin drastically overshot his goal by conquering not only the Mongol tribes, but amassed an empire never before seen on earth. In 1206 A.D. he was coroneted with the name Genghis Khan, which literally translates to 'Universal Ruler'. Even though he internally felt spiritually driven, his ruthlessness on the battlefield revealed his internal conflict, notoriously observed by his enemies. Although his armies caused broad destruction, murder and mercilessness, Genghis Khan struggled to preserve a reverence and respect for teachers, philosophers and trades folk. Ironically, Khan loathed the aristocracy and reserved the majority of his anger for them. He was also one of the few early conquerors who allowed religious freedoms within his kingdom (38) (39).

Can the same trinity describing human behavior be applied to all nature? Yes. We need to look no further than the forces in nature. One of the most familiar instances is the force of gravity. From a young age most school children are taught that gravity is what holds us to the ground. What goes up must come down. When we jump up, we fall back to earth. (*Note: humans did modify this absolute rule with the advent of space flight! It turned out to be only a conditional and relative rule.*) Gravity is the measurable attractive force between all masses. The nature of gravity allows the earth to sustain its mass and not fall apart into the reaches of space. Therefore, gravity sustains the status quo, and keeps the world as we know it, knitted together. It creates what science calls *inertia*, or resistance to change much like Vishnu or the Watcher behavior.

For people fortunate enough to have the rights to a high school education or higher, we also learn in physics or astronomy that gravity is responsible for, not only the creation of our solar system from cosmic gasses and dust, but all stars numbering in the trillions throughout the known Universe. The act of gasses coming together from stellar distances and creating our Sun is one of the most dramatic and energetic creations known, a true miracle of the Universe. Therefore gravity definitely exhibits the Maker behavior. Think about it. The Sun is the greatest source of energy, heat and light near our planet. Furthermore, the Sun is handedly responsible for the unique environment that has sustained life *as* we know it and even *before* we knew it here on Earth. We owe our very lives to the Sun's existence as well as the unique conditions of the planet we stand on. It is no surprise that the ancient Egyptians held special reverence for the Sun as the king of their pantheon of gods, known as Ra.

Within the Universe, many dramatic examples of creation, such as galaxies and nebula offer proof of gravity's ability to behave like a force of creation, like Hinduisms Brahma. The sheer magnitude of gravity's creative power is more awe inspiring than humanities greatest Makers.

Finally, gravity hides a dramatic destructor side as well. More advanced education in astrophysics teaches how massive forces of gravity play a role in supernovas, black holes and galactic centers. Similar to living creatures, even the mightiest of stars must fall and fall they do. In fact, the saying the bigger they are the harder they fall could not be better stated. The more massive a star begins, the more violent and destructive the star's end. The largest class stars, ably named *red giants*, undergo a massive explosion followed by a massive *implosion* where the star collapses inward. These implosions continue with such force that the red giant shrinks down in size becoming a highly massive singularity where "... matter is crushed to infinite density, the pull of gravity is infinitely strong, and space-time has infinite curvature..." (40). In other words, there is an infinite mass with infinite gravity at a single point which science calls a black hole. This stellar void is so violent and destructive that all mass (and assumed information) within a certain distance known as the 'event horizon' including light is pulled in. The dramatically large change in gravitational force, based on the distance from the black hole center, is called the gravitational gradient. This gravitational gradient will literally tear apart anything from end to end, molecule to molecule and atom to atom. As far as astronomers can tell, the only thing left is massive amounts of gamma energy that escapes to balance the conversion of mass to energy. So even in the most extreme case, energy survives, since it cannot be created or destroyed, a scientific law called '*conservation of energy*'. A black hole is the most dramatic example of demolisher behavior observed by man, and fits very well with the Śhiva symbolism in Hindu culture.

It is easy to argue these same themes played out in many areas of nature and human behavior. People who study the bible can find the same symbolic references even when referring to the biblical God. The book of Genesis, in the Old Testament, refers to the "Lord" which is a personification of the creator or Maker. Whether this idea was borrowed from earlier Middle East or Eastern cultures, such as Brahma, Osiris, or other pantheon patron deities is of some debate. However, such discussions are often simply a human conflict over bragging rights and consequently unimportant in the grand scheme of things.

Not too long after the creation event, according to biblical scripture, God shifted priorities and decided upon the destruction path. This manifestation is the wrathful God of the Old Testament taking the name "Lord God" (41). Stories of the great flood, destruction of cities for their vices populate the Old Testament, seen by both Christian and Jewish faiths as the 'Word' of historical truth, regardless of much evidence that suggests these stories were 'borrowed' from earlier religions and cultures.

Then there is prophesying about a great prophet that will deliver the 'chosen few', according to the bible, that will be delivered from the end of days (wrathful godhead reference).

Sadly, today's conflicts around the world by the three largest monotheistic religions fight, kill and war over this basic point. Who is this deliverer? Have they already come; and who then are the chosen?

Christians feel from the depth of their hearts that Jesus Christ is that person and furthermore is the 'Son of God'. The 'Lord Jesus Christ' fulfills the role of Vishnu, the one who sustains life, balances and forgives all sins, which inadvertently allows many of this faith to sit idle as Watchers. If you have casual conversation with a divisive evangelical Christian, not only will they tell you more than you asked for, but they may feel compelled to save you as well. If you refuse, a zealous few may even boldly tell you they are sorry that you will be damned for all eternity despite them knowing entirely nothing about your character, nature, history, morality or sense of right and wrong.

I should pause here, because I was brought up in the Christian faith, originally as Catholic and later in less traditional versions. I know the feelings and compulsions that are taught to youth from a place of experience, not of observation. What I realized then, as I know now, there are tremendous amounts of beautifully moral and wonderful people outside this fundamentalist viewpoint of Christian faith. Although, Christianity has many admirable traditions such as compassion, aiding those less fortunate and mercy among 'sinners', I have also witnessed outright bigotry, self-righteousness and plain ignorance of truth in the most fundamentalist and conservative sects of Christian faiths.

The Jewish faith recognizes Christ as a great prophet and acknowledge his contributions to modern monotheistic beliefs, but don't recognize him as the 'deliverer'. Islamists, who it should be noted, have just as many varieties as their Christian and Jewish brothers, look more simply to the prophet Mohammed as the one true prophet. This complex story of religious proselytizing is nowhere near complete, if you don't account for the billions whom practice Buddhist, Hindu, or other spiritual traditions.

It is truly tragic that we as a global society have not come to terms with this fighting over who lays claim to the best belief story. All can agree that prehistorical and historical evidence discovered through study, scientific discovery and reflection point to a single obvious truth. We are all here on this little planet together. We have been here longer than we have scriptures to tell us how we and all life emerged on this planet. Therefore, for us to survive in a world that is getting smaller by the second, we need to work together. We need to put our minds, souls and resources to solving the problems that threaten the only home we know, Earth.

In this book, we are exploring the balance between a path toward enlightened thought and creative forces inspiring us within. It is in this space where new possibilities exist that benefit us all. It is in this spirit; the scientific renaissance dawned revealing divine beauty through discovery and our connection with it.

Our exploration of spirituality has merged with the path of scientific discovery. It is at this nexus that humankind will expand its spiritual evolvement. Let's now closely examine what science has to say about the universe we inhabit and ultimately our spiritual connection with it.

PART II:

REBUILDING A SPIRITUAL THEORY USING INTEGRATIVE SCIENCE

CHAPTER 5
DIVINE BEAUTY
IN DISCOVERY

I am among those who think that science has great beauty. A scientist in his laboratory is not only a technician: he is also a child placed before natural phenomena which impress him like a fairy tale.

-Marie Curie (1867 – 1934; discoverer of Radium)

SCIENCE-BREAKING THROUGH THE DOGMA

Ask a Nobel Prize winning scientist how they felt when they discovered a major breakthrough that changed the way they thought about the universe. If they have a spiritual bone in their body, they may tell you they felt a wave of emotion, or had an indescribable epiphany or perhaps even felt like they had touched the mind of the Source with a sense of communion and understanding. Even Albert Einstein wanted to "...understand the mind of God..."

As we explore a compilation of scientific discoveries in Chapter 5, don't be concerned about completely understanding every element of the science. After all, some scientists spend an entire lifetime trying to understand some of these concepts! Instead, pay attention to how each discovery contributes to a new spiritual model forged from scientific knowledge and noetic discovery rather than fabrication and fairy tales.

As we briefly examined previously, we are all suggestible

and often convinced of teachings and dogma acquired over the years from others. Much of the information we receive is valid and useful.

- 1 + 1 = 2 (most of the time)

- Make sure you drink plenty of water or you will get dehydrated

- Play nice with others

- Do not fight (most of the time)

Although typically given with good intentions, a large portion of knowledge we receive is freely open to validation, questioning and testing. Be wary of any individual, institution or government who tells you otherwise, as they may have some special interest in you not validating the information to your satisfaction.

So the question becomes, how do we sift through the mountains of information we are taught at schools, universities, churches, synagogues, temples, governments and companies? Most of the time it is a non issue because our younger self, sometimes referred to as the inner child naturally questions and desires to test things. The problem occurs when our curiosity is quenched or suppressed by outside forces.

Being a father of three boys, I completely understand some of the parental reasons to limit you children's curiosity due to the potential for danger or personal harm befalling the child. However, I must admit there is something to be said for the 'law of natural consequences'. What quicker and more efficient way for little Jimmy to learn to not climb on the dog. The dog either nips at little Jimmy (as she would to her own pups) or gets up to walk away and Jimmy falls to the ground and bonks his head. Either way, little Jimmy learns to not climb on the dog.

Now this may seem a bit harsh, but that is the way human beings and animals are wired and have been since the dawn of life on this planet. Neuroscience has numerous studies confirming that the fastest learning response in animals and humans is via pain. The second fastest is through reward. This is why hyper-protective parents, who are trying to prevent all harm from befalling their child by not allowing him or her to participate, are actually stunting their child's natural learning patterns. In the recent past, parenting was more of an active observer role rather than playing interference with any potential danger. Let's examine a child and a hot pot.

1. Touch finger to hot pot.
2. Get burned!
3. Lesson: Do not touch hot pot!
4. Repeat if necessary (not usually necessary).
5. Done!

Congratulations! Your child has become a bona fide amateur empirical scientist! Obviously, certain experiments are justifiably not allowed for kids. For example, "Let's jump in front of Mommy's moving car to surprise her and see what happens." Therefore always temper free range learning with wisdom. If you would like more information, I suggest a good book called, *"Free Range Kids"* by Lenore Skenazy, which logically covers what age appropriate freedom is for kids in this modern age.

Think on it. We as children tested, questioned and explored everything our hungry little minds could get our literal hands on. Our parents and grandparents generations did even more so. It was not until preschool, religious school or kindergarten that we were told to keep our curious little 'hands', and by extension minds, to ourselves. Completely shutting down a child at this age has detrimental effects on their creativity, imagination and ability to dissect the truth. In fact more and more educational research shows that young children mentally flourish with MORE HANDS ON EDUCATION!

This fundamental philosophy is behind the well established Montessori teaching system. Dr. Mary Montessori, an Italian scientist and pediatric physician, began working in a psychiatric clinic in Rome about a century ago. Dr. Montessori's initial hands on experiment using sensory-rich environments showed that children previously labeled by society as "deficient and insane" were able to pass Italy's public schools standardized testing within two years! These were astonishing results, since the dogma of the time (and even until recently at many universities) was students learn best when being lectured (fed) the 'correct' information. Did Mary listen to this? No, she recognized the truth that the status quo educational system failed this demographic of children. She refused to accept this *de facto* standard as the only result and thus created an alternative. (42)

From that inspirational result, Montessori pushed forward to rediscover the way all children and people are wired to learn. She opened "A Children's House" for pre-school children living among the slums of San Lorenzo and discovered that children learn best by doing *purposeful activity*. Those that were just fed information, the way many classrooms still do to this day, learned far less, their behavior was less positive and their ability to have long term focus did not compare to the kids receiving high sensory *purposeful activity*.

Dr. Montessori once wrote, *"Whoever touches the life of the child touches the most sensitive point of a whole, which has roots in the most distant past and climbs toward the infinite future."*

Since Dr. Montessori's death in 1952, Montessori based programs have flourished in the Europe and the United States. Certified Montessori schools, teachers and training is organized through non-profit firms such as the American Montessori Society (AMS). A 2006 article in *Science* by Angeline Lillard and Nicole Else-Quest compared traditional public school and Montessori based schools in the performance of 5 year olds and 12 year olds. The results statistically showed that, "...Montessori education fosters social and academic skills that are equal or superior to those fostered by a pool of other types of schools." In addition, the study found a significant reduction of "ambiguous rough play", such as wrestling without smiling, in the Montessori trained kids than the traditional public schools. (43)

The above illustration shows the power of challenging dogma, in this case, conventional educational practices, using scientific methods and finding a better solution based upon facts. Just because someone told you a particular way of doing something is best, does not make it so. Evidence and results will declare something true or untrue. Notice the parallel that *purposeful activity* has with our earlier discussions of purpose and playing an active role in your own spiritual evolution.

Finally, notice a more subtle surprise from the data. Kids of ages 3-12 all performed better, learned better, appeared more morally responsible and had more positive social strategies and connections when their predominant practice throughout the day was *purposeful activity*. Purposeful activity is literally "activity with a purpose". For those who don't have children in a Montessori program, one of the features is for kids to work on an activity for prolonged periods of time as long as the child feels compelled to keep learning using that activity. Does this not echo the same purpose we are discussing with relation to aligning your *purposeful activity* with your spirit? Perhaps the reason these children excel so well is because they felt a calling to explore a particular activity on counting cubes one day, sounds of letters the next and caterpillar larva on the third day.

Therefore, I throw out this hypothesis for you to explore. *If you take time every day, however small, and pursue a purposeful activity in alignment with Source; you will become a more whole, morally balanced and happy human being.*

Test this hypothesis and let me know how it goes at my website www.drchadkennedy.com. Challenge what you think you know. See how it affects your life. If it appears to pan out, encourage your children, friends and neighbors to do the same. Insight #7 below is the giving gift.

> **Insight #7: Take time each day to focus on a purposeful activity in alignment with Source.**

LOGIC: A WAY TO SPIRITUAL BALANCE

> *-Logic is the handmaiden to humanity's conscious spirit. Without her, we would be truly lost, ever searching for that which can fill the void.-*

Logic seems, to many of us, more like fuzzy logic, a concept rather than a concrete idea. The English term 'logic' is derived from the original Greek feminine of *logos*, or *logikē*, meaning reason. Interestingly, ancient Greek philosophy believed that *logos* or reason is divine wisdom and the controlling principle in the Universe. *How is it today, so much of humanity is not aware of this relationship between logic and divine wisdom?* Did ancient Greeks know better than people today? Logic is as fundamental to understanding the divine events in the Universe as it is to probe the mundane. In fact, Greeks made no distinction between the two, yet in our modern ignorant glory, humanity has, in large part, forgotten this fundamental principle known eons ago. Many people choose to close their eyes to truth presented all around them. Sadly, others have few tools, with which to properly use logic, to reveal the daily miracles surrounding them. A sun burst, star light from light years away, the birth of a galaxy, the budding of a maple seed, the making of an idea, the flight of a bumble bee, the movement of a flock of geese; all of these things are miracles of nature that have been revealed through the use of logic. If living a spiritual existence means experiencing beauty in all of its forms, then logic is required to 'see'.

Insight #8: We know far less about how things are in the Universe than we don't know.

Logic and trained minds help us navigate this fantastic landscape, to truly discover for ourselves, what is really going on. Logic is the fundamental pillar of all scientific inquiry today. Anyone who studies a topic long enough, makes a significant contribution to a body of knowledge and successfully defends it, using logic in the form of scientific method, can attain a Doctorate in Philosophy or PhD. Interestingly; there are many scientists who are adamant about separating their scientific study results from any holistic logical or spiritual model of the Universe. However, I suggest that these are the exact types of people who are uniquely qualified to pursue such scientific endeavors by critically testing hypothesis about physical connections with the spiritual.

It used to be, lack of education, access to information and literacy prevented much of humanity from studying connections between spirituality and progressive of thought, knowledge and wisdom. Now it seems whole segments of society, starved of any real connection by repressive pressures and dogma, are blindly choosing to ignore the greater Universe in which they are an integral part. Instead these people choose to listen to folks that have little to no training in areas of logic for their spiritual guidance. Albert Einstein succinctly stated at a Symposium on Science, Philosophy and Religion in 1941, "*Science without religion is lame. Religion without science is blind.*" Even Einstein knew of the important connection between science and spirituality. More importantly, he understood the rigor in which to pursue future questions on these connections.

The basic ability to reason and make conclusions based upon what is presented uses forms of logic. Without logic, we would be no better off than our primate ancestors or birds working from instinct. Modern humans' very ability to adapt and progress for tens of thousands of years would have never occurred. The wheel never used. Fire never harnessed for warmth. Civilizations never created.

If we ignore logic and science all together there is a significant danger of regressing into a new dark age. We, individually and as a society, would fall to the whims of nature and become slaves to those who choose to think for us. Without conscious ability to be able to think and take responsible actions, we would no longer be Makers of our destiny; thus, spirituality without logic becomes indeed, '*blind*'.

The counter argument is just as important, if we only hold to logic without purposeful and spiritual alignment, we collectively lose ourselves in a chaotic abyss. Without purpose, we immerse ourselves in a virtual maelstrom of competing random thoughts, ideas and evidence leading nowhere, a void. Therefore, spiritual alignment and purpose are the glue that holds our collective logical pathways together, thereby progressing toward a common universal path. To demonstrate this effect try the following group experiment.

1. Take a long piece of thread or rope and cut it into equal lengths (~ about 1 meter each).
2. Make sure that the pieces are long enough to tie one end to an object (e.g. metal rod, PVC pipe or wood) or tie them all together at one end.
3. Clear an area for the activity.
4. Make sure you have one puller for every string or rope.
5. Have one or more outside observers noting what happens.
6. Have everyone close their eyes or use blindfolds before beginning.

7. On the count of 3 (or 4 if you like) pull in random directions and at random times on the object or knot.
8. Have the observers note what happens.
9. Now give them a purpose or objective, such as, move the object ten feet to the west or lift the object off the ground and place it on a table.
10. Have the group try again with the suggested purpose in mind and see what results.
11. Share experiences, sensations and feelings that occurred during the activity.

RELIGION RESISTS CHANGE, SPIRITUALITY EMBRACES CHANGE

> *Science has proof without any certainty. Creationists have certainty without any proof.*
>
> *-Ashley Montague (1905- 1999; world renown anthropologist)*

As we expand on the idea of spirituality being in alignment with scientific and logical practices, I need to clarify a distinction between religion and spiritually.

Religion as I have defined in previous chapters is a belief system organized under the banner of an institution. Typically these organizations, regardless of type, survive on the ability of their members to place money in the hands of the organization. As long as member donations are voluntary, such contributions are commendable and expected since all organizations, governments, companies, provinces, states and so on operate in a similar manner. Problems occur with institutions requiring contributions similar to magazine or gym memberships, if you don't pay you don't belong. From experience, people understand that group solidarity can accomplish much more when efforts are channeled and focused with the power of numbers behind these efforts. A great deal of good and progress can come from such a structured system, and we will look at scientific research that supports this concept in spiritual terms later in the book. The problems begin to occur when these institutions take it upon themselves to dictate to its members *how to think* and *how to believe.* Once a group has you comfortable with them calling the shots for your mind and body, why not have them manage your spirit, essence, energy or soul. Some institutions promote the idea that only true salvation, enlightenment or a blissful afterlife can come through them **exclusively**. This is the most ancient form of fear mongering and control that has survived throughout mankind's existence.

Let's walk through a hypothetical thought experiment. A salesman comes to your door in the middle of the evening and says to you, "For 10% of everything you earn, I have an insurance policy that guarantees that you will live forever in enlightened bliss. You will get to hang out with as many angels as you can imagine." Some salesmen may tempt you with the Premium Martyr (PM) Policy, "If you act now by sacrificing your life to our cause, we will guarantee that you can hang out with thousands of drop dead (pun intended) gorgeous virgins who have nothing better to do than to wait on you. Just sign here and we will start automatically drawing 10% from your account or all your possessions if you want the PM policy."

The unspoken fine print states, "if you ever change your mind, want to make modifications, change the amount, or deviate from the contract in any way, the whole guarantee will be null and void. However, we will keep trying to get funds from you to make up for our losses." The salesman then lets you briefly leaf through a copy of the hundreds or thousands of pages of fine print (Bible, Quran, Book of Mormon or other text) which he would also be happy to sell to you, your friends and family if you like.

What would you say? Many of us would say, "No way! You cannot make that guarantee, you are just a salesman."

A cautious few, who are perhaps interested in learning more would say, "Well let me read through your documentation first and I will get back with you at my convenience and let you know. Do you have a card, proof of heavenly contracts executed (no pun intended), nirvana references of happy afterlife customers or assets and credentials that show me that your institution can keep up your end of the deal? The last thing I want to do is wake up after dying and realize that you did not reserve my cloud condo in Paradise, and instead I am in a place called Motel Hell, in the Inferno, because you had the wrong instruction manual or did not forward the payments, prayers and good works to the right address. What proof do you have?"

Instead, most of us sadly, myself included, trusted the salesman, took what he or she said at face value and unconsciously signed the contract for our mind, body and soul without ever having read the entire fine print or having had the opportunity to do so independently.

It gets uglier; most of us unintentionally agreed to this contract long before we could read, write or even reliably go to the restroom by ourselves. We were children when this deal was thrust upon us without our signature. As such, even when we could start reading and writing, the fine print was being 'interpreted' for us by the very same salesman or institution for which he or she works. Fortunately, since we did not actually sign our soul away, there is still hope for all of us.

I am not against voluntarily making an adult decision to join a particular group, but it should be well thought out with no punitive damages when things don't work out. I give a lot of credit to belief systems that allow their young people to take a hiatus from the contract when they 'come of age' and start making discriminating thoughts about what to believe and why. However, there comes a day of reckoning. For example, the Hamish allow their children to come back if they knowingly agree to the strict lifestyle, traditions and belief system. I personally, don't agree with their beliefs, but I do believe their concept of allowing their children to explore and find their own personal connection with the divine is a good start. The down side is, if the young adult rejects Hamish beliefs, they must also leave behind their friends and family they love and grew up with, a literal excommunication. Many religious practices have evoked excommunication pressures such as these to create a zero sum game with their 'flock'. Catholicism and Mormonism are two distinct religions that have or had the practice. If they cannot make you conform by choice or fear, then the institution pressures compliance by guilt or threat of banishment.

If society allows religious institutions to govern our every action, then we are in real danger of becoming a fanatical system similar to extreme church-state governments in the Middle East. A dramatic, yet potent, example is the fundamentalist Afghan group, the Taliban. The Taliban doctrine promotes a society where women are, in their 'religious interpretation', justifiably beat or tortured. In the case of Bibi Aisha (Miss Aisha), a newly married 18 year old Afghan girl, the Taliban cut off her nose and ears for fleeing her prearranged abusive husband and in-laws (Search the links, below). The Taliban acted as trial, judge and jury to enact their 'religiously justified' sentence. This act was seen by the world at large as so inhumane, that this brave girl allowed Jodi Bieber, an outside photo journalist, to take her picture which dons the controversial August 1st 2010 TIME magazine cover in hopes that such a fate would not befall other women. Take a moment to see this cover at TIME.com (http://www.time.com/time/world/

article/0,8599,2007238,00.html) or view the video interview with Jodi Bieber at (http://www.time.com/time/video/player/0,32068 ,294175100001_2007267,00.html).

You can also simply go to www.time.com and search for the term "Aisha Cover" on their search tool. The photograph depicts 18 year old Aisha of Afghanistan as a plea to the US and other countries to seriously consider the moral obligation to champion and ensure the rights of abused women and to consider what legacy the US leaves behind in the wake of war.

The founding fathers of the United States had a keen sense of religion's potential abuse of power and accordingly placed balancing measures within the fabric of the constitution to prohibit the government of the free-thinking people of America to favor any religion over another. Religious freedom without favoritism is one of the great pillars of American values. The Taliban example presents exactly why. Sure, you may like the idea if your particular faith is in power, but don't think for a second that governing by religious doctrine instead of a system ruled by educated, free people is not corruptible. Remember, when entities are threatened, they will fight tooth and nail to remain in existence. Even now the Taliban is fighting for relevance in a country that is allowing, for the first time in decades, women to be educated and participate in the political process despite the Taliban's disapproving eyes. Think of the spiritual foresight the writers of the US constitution had when you examine the provocative picture of Aisha and imagine if this was your daughter.

In addition, other women are stoned to death, stripped of all their ownership or even their children if they so much as hint at divorcing an abusive spouse. This is the terrible reality in Afghanistan in the year 2010, not a theoretical concept.

In contrast to a church-state enforced or religious doctrine, personal spirituality is the *individual connection* and expression with the divine. It dwells in profound knowing that you are part of a greater whole, beyond mere imagination or control. There is no salesman telling you what you can and cannot do, can and cannot believe. There are no short cuts in spiritual development, no free passes to those who donate enough money, no buy one salvation and all is forgiven for you and your family, no VIP cards and no frequent prayer miles club. Spiritual development requires attention, listening, energy, dedication, courage, perseverance, logic, contemplation, meditation and often sacrifices to achieve progress. Until we know otherwise, there is no guarantee of an exclusive all expense paid vacation to paradise upon death of this body. All we have, thus far is a notion and preliminary evidence suggesting there is more to this existence than this human form.

So why on Earth take this path? Simply, it may be a calling. For others it is the desire to seek out truth. And for many it is to understand and know the universal connection that binds us to the grand tapestry of life. It is a compelling moral and ethical passion in the present that one finds bliss. It is the evolving path between you and the divine Universe, no middle man required; hence the reason many define the process as *spiritual evolution.*

> *Insight#9: No one on this planet has any authority over your mind and spirit, no middleman to divine insight, only teachers that aid along The Way. We are all students first, teachers second.*

This distinction between spirituality and religion, and institutional tendencies for self preservation, lead us to see that organized institutions of religion resist change, even if in the long run, that very change may validate them. *Spirituality, defined in this manner, is the process of becoming connected and aligned with The Way, an eastern expression for a process or path of enlightened existence, rather than a state of being.* Thus spirituality is at its very essence, transformation. It is not hindered by the anchors of tradition and dogmatic viewpoints; and thus, flows as easy as a dandelion seed in the winds of change.

CHANGE

> *-Life does not exist without motion; motion does not exist without change; thus without change life does not exist-*

At first glance change may not seem to be a spirit-knowledge connecting concept. Furthermore, fundamental *change* is probably one of the most difficult and misunderstood concepts to grasp for humans. We are preconditioned to think of the World and Universe as a series of objects or entities. We then break down these larger objects into smaller structures made up of particular states of matter. For example, I am a human being with two arms, two legs, a torso and a head with which it appears, I think. I sit in a chair, which stands on the floor. The floor is connected to a home in my city or town and on and on. However, this state model of existence completely misses the real story going on behind the scenes. Here is the key. Quantum physics reveals that the 'states' of a static objects are an illusion. Reality lies within the rules by which we change the states.

If we are merely the sum of our material parts, such as a house is the sum of all of its construction materials, then I am no different than the house. If a city is the sum of the buildings, machines and people that it consists of, then it is no better or worse than any other city of similar makeup and size. What these descriptions don't pay attention to is the *quality, dynamics or change* that is occurring in these systems.

Here is a thought experiment. Are you the same person that you were yesterday? What if we expand the dimension of time? Are you the same person that you were five years ago? Ten years ago? At birth? You probably answered a resounding no. Why?

The answer is *Change*. Specifically, you are a completely different version or model of yourself than you were even a few years ago. How do I know? Most of your cells, the very basic building block of your body have long since died. You are a collective living descendant evolved over hundreds of generations of cellular reproduction. These very cells, their molecular, ion and atomic constituents have been exchanged continuously with your environment without your knowledge or consent for the better part of your life. This same fact is true with every living system on the planet. Therefore it is safe to say that none of us are the sum of our components since all of us have traded, destroyed or recycled our fundamental building blocks multiple times throughout our lifetime. We are literally changing into a different person each day. The irony is, regardless of this ever changing transformation of our bodies, we still recall our former selves and have stored memories, knowledge and wisdom from each transformative version. We will revisit this topic later.

An interesting paradox about the word *Change*, it can be a noun that describes an action which by English definition is a verb. It literally means 'alteration, difference or transformation.' If we are not the sum of our parts and are instead beings of change, how does one then perceive this change? In 1899, the eminent physicist, Max Planck, theoretically created natural minimal units based on free space for several phenomenon including time. *Planck time*, t_p, as it is called, is defined as the amount of time for light to travel 1 Planck unit of distance in a vacuum or approximately 5.39124×10^{-44} s. This is considered to be the smallest possible observable time since nothing (as we know it) travels faster than the speed of light.

How does Planck time apply to change? Let's assume the Universe is like a computer that runs at the fastest clock speed imaginable, *'Planck Clock Frequency'* or $f_p = 1/t_p \cong 1.85486 \times 10^{19}$ YHz. In more simple terms that is about 18.5 Million Trillion Trillion Trillion computations per second, far faster than any subsystem within the Universe is known to clock at! For comparison, the fastest electronic computer processors as of December, 2010 run up to 5.2 GHz (5.2 Billion computations per second) for the IBM zEnterprise 196 mainframe cores. Yet with all this speed our electronic systems don't come close to the amount of computational *capacity* of the human mind.

With all this computational ability in our brain, humans can only cognitively process as fast as their conscious perception. That does not mean that we are unable to process faster. However, if we expect to consciously be aware of a change of events then we are limited by the speed of human perception. For example, the human eye is arguably the fastest information transfer pathway into the human brain via light transduction. Although our computer screens run at about 60 – 75 Hz (60-75 screen updates per second for a modern progressive scan LCD screen), we don't consciously notice the transitions of states on the screen. At best humans can consciously notice visual changes on the time scale order of ~100 -200 milliseconds. Therefore actual Change on the Universal timescale is unperceivable to humans and computers alike.

In essence, there are no such objects perceivable as states of the system at Planck's time scale. There is then, the continuous flow of causal interactions, or flow of cause and effect, and motions at the Planck scale or quantum level. Quantum time is blurred. Thus, from one instant to the next all that is you is ever transforming. *Never will you be exactly as you are now, even in the instant that you just read this sentence!* You are continuously becoming different, evolving toward something new.

Even if you subscribe to Buddhist traditions where the state of Samadhi, or the state of pure observation without attachment, is a desirable achievement, one still observes change. Through the act of observing, we change and learn as a result.

Likewise, your loved ones, city, country along with the entire Universe around you are also changing. Existence is never the same from one instant, or quantum of time, to the next. Therefore, change is not something to be feared, it occurs all around us whether we like it or not, so it is better to be aware of it and embrace that it is a fundamental part of your being.

> *Insight#10: We consciously and continually observe change not quantum states.*

QUANTUM CONUNDRUMS

How do we know Insight #10 is true? Quantum physics has proven it with countless experiments over the last century. All 'matter' whether it is atoms, molecules, rocks, trees, air, water, gold, cows, fish and even humans are made of the same raw materials. Most educated cultures around the World stop their general populace science education at the atomic level with chemistry. However, nuclear and quantum physics peeled back several more layers of the 'matter onion' below the scale of chemistry. Physicists discovered and verified all kinds of subatomic components such as, photons, leptons, alpha particles, beta particles, muons, and six types of quarks. Below that each quark has its own color and anti-particle version. Therefore if we are to build a better model of spirituality, perhaps it would benefit humanity to better understand what makes up the known Universe in hopes of shedding light on the unknown spiritual Universe.

My goal in this book is to reveal the common edges of science and spiritualism not to teach a hundred years of scientific discovery and justification. Therefore, I refer interested readers to other books and resources on the intricacies of matter. In this chapter, my aim is to bring forward major implications of such discoveries, as they pertain to alignment with spiritually, logic and life. Part of the difficulty for people wading through this material is that even the most rigorous physicists are human and as such, they are prone to current and historical passionate disagreements as in any discipline.

For example, change through the eyes of a quantum physicist is the transition between unknowable states. Early contributors to quantum mechanics, Werner Heisenberg and Erwin Schrödinger, suggested change is not perceivable, measurable or knowable if you are looking at the state of a particle or thing. For example, if you know the location of an electron, or its state, you cannot measure its velocity, or change in position in time. The reverse is also true. In addition, they believed that the state of everything is an enormous set of probabilities for all possible states of a particle or by extension an object (44). Therefore, they concurred with the famous Niels Bohr, father of the atomic model that the path of the particle or object in question did not exist in what we know as reality.

This irked Albert Einstein to say the least, because it implied that momentum (a measure of a particles mass multiplied by its path or change of position in an instant in time, $\mathbf{H}=m*\mathbf{v}$) would not exist if the particles location was known and vice versa. In addition, all possibilities exist for all particles, thereby making all objects possibilities composed of these particles possible. In other words a DNA molecule, cat, tree, human or even a solar system would exist in between states of infinite number of possibilities, simultaneously. How then, do we observe only one of these possibilities and understand it from a human experience?

The interpretation is that the possible states only collapse to what we experience as reality when *the infinite potential of matter is measured or observed*. **Another way to think about this concept is, all possibilities of the entire Universe exist at every interval (change) between states (instants) and our act of observation (measurement) brings the Universe as we perceive it into being.**

For years Einstein and Bohr would heatedly debate this issue until it appeared that Bohr and the quantum physicists had won the day. However, it was not until physicists John von Neuman and later Eugene Wigner modified quantum physics to include a solution suggesting not everything is random changes or 'roles of the cosmic dice'. Quantum physics coined the term, *quantum coherent collapsible event* (QCCE) to describe the observer effect of collapsing all things into knowable states in the Universe from infinite possibilities. Simply, this interpretation creates the need for an observer to describe the fabric of the Universe. The interpretation implies that in order for knowable changes in reality to occur from moment to moment, observers are required to create these collapsible events.

If this conclusion sounds confusing, don't worry, you are in good company! The point is that quantum physics suggests that conscious observation, presumably by a sentient interpreter, is required for reality to materialize. That appears as quite a lofty statement for science to make and suggests a 'special' vantage for those that can observe. Even quantum physicists cannot quite agree on the interpretation of these experimental findings. Quantum Mechanics has four main interpretations to the above phenomenon; the Copenhagen Interpretation (that of Bohr's origins); the Stochastic Ensemble Interpretation; the Relative State Interpretation (Many Worlds-Multiverse) and the Hidden Variable Interpretation. Since thousands of articles have been written over the past 60 years debating which interpretation is correct by many serious physicists, I could not possibly summarize all of the opinions and experiments here without overtaking the entire purpose of the book. However, I summarize the fundamental ideas with the following:

1. Matter exists as a statistical probability function (Heisenberg Uncertainty and Schrödinger Wave-probability function) with all options of location and momentum available.
2. Matter only takes on specific location, momentum and form when observed by an 'observer'. (Debatably an outside measurement system such as you or me).
3. Because we affect all matter by our mere observation, we (the observers) influence and to a limited extent creatively control in the Universe

The conclusions are very inviting and have become the siren songs of many physicists and spiritual personalities alike. Who would not want to live in a Universe that you can control by will. It would be like waking up and discovering that you are truly in the Hollywood movie *The Matrix* and can manipulate it like Neo. However, no one, me included, has reportedly found this extraordinary power to do whatever they cosmically wish and for good reason. The potential consequences of any human being having that level of control over reality would be subject to corruption and devastating to life as we know it. Shockingly, science has revealed, that the assumption that we do subtly *influence* reality is true! There are hundreds of studies that have shown that people singly or as groups **can** affect matter, electronics and society in significant ways. However, the effects appear limited, but are far more statistically significant than, for example, the 'compelling' study past through the FDA decades ago that justified taking an aspirin a day to prevent cardiovascular disease. Obviously more research needs to be done, but the evidence of human intention and perhaps more affecting the Universe around us is tantalizing to say the least (45) (46) (47).

In contrast to this evidence, there are a growing number of physicists, engineers and scientists who question the fundamental assumptions of Quantum Mechanics. Perhaps one of the most unorthodox and notable is the work of Dr. Randell L. Mills M.D., founder of BlackLight Power Inc. (BLP). His company has a team of scientists, experimental physicists and engineers researching, modeling, designing and building what they call Hydrino Reactors. More information on the Hydrino Reactor technology, theories, software and a three volume book can be found at www.blacklightpower.com. As a Harvard School of Medicine graduate, Dr. Mills originally discovered the Hydrino catalytic reaction by accident and fortunately had a diverse enough background in Magnetic Resonance (MR), electrical engineering and chemistry to recognize something unusual was occurring. What makes the reaction so extraordinary is the amount of energy (heat) released. In a continuous reaction, 1.3-6.5 times more energy is released than any previously known chemical reaction. The most energetic chemical reaction is combustion of two H_2 and one O_2 to form two H_2O molecules, or water. These results were independently replicated and verified by a research team lead by Dr. K.V. Ramanujachary at Rowan University in Glassboro, New Jersey. According to Dr. Mills, a portable Hydrino generator can theoretically fuel a car for 5000 miles on a gallon of water, be removed, plugged into your electrical panel at home and have enough power left over to power your neighborhood. The system is less energetic than nuclear fission or fusion, but is reportedly far more stable and controllable. This result fundamentally means that something is happening that has never been explained by physics before.

Since its inception, the BlackLight Power team found the reaction creates a new form of transiently stable, low energy hydrogen. This type of matter is called, a Hydrino. By Mill's definition, a hydrino is similar to a hydrogen atom in most respects except that the minimal orbit radius of the electron shell is smaller than previously thought. In quantum mechanics (QM) we call this shell the K shell with a quantum number, n, equal to 1. Traditional QM tells us that the orbital quantum number, n, can only be an integer greater than or equal to 1 (i.e. n = 1, 2, 3, etc.). GEN3 Partners, an independent research group, subsequently tested 'hydrinos' and verified a light signature with cutoffs of 22.8 nm and 10.1 nm, well below Hydrogen's QM predicted minimum of 80 nm when n=1. The evidence of Mill's experiments and others conflicted with traditional quantum mechanics leading to questions about the fundamental assumptions of QM. Specifically, Dr. Mills questions one of the sacred cows of QM, Schrödinger's wave-probability function, which we discussed previously. Schrödinger assumed that as the radius of an electron approaches infinity ($r_e \rightarrow \infty$), the probability of the charge at that radius approaches 0 ($\Psi \rightarrow 0$). The Schrödinger assumption gave rise to a variety of postulates about electrons and all other particles built upon this foundation, suggesting the particle has a probability of being essentially anywhere. From a physical-spiritual model perspective, this assumption has dramatic implications which we will entangle ourselves with later, but for now I want you to be aware of this pivotal assumption.

Also remember, QM postulates, backed by decades of supporting evidence, that in order for a particle to locate in a particular space-time (location in three dimensional space at a specific time), an observer (such as you or I) is required to collapse the wave-probability functions to that location. Thus everything that we as humans consciously observe, see, hear, taste, smell and touch exists technically everywhere as a possibility prior to our conscious awareness which collapses everything into place.

Mill's is researching the evidence against this assumption and simply applies Maxwell's Equations (which reliably predict electronic and electricity use in the modern world) as a boundary condition so that particles, such as the electron, have a closed radius, r_e, instead of Schrödinger's infinite radius conclusion. Evidence for this electron radius limit has been repeatedly measured in free electrons in super fluid helium.

As you are hopefully beginning to see, even science disciplines build dogmatic thinking over time, similar to their religious counterparts. The main difference is science continuously allows questioning of fundamental assumptions creating an environment for modifications and continuous improvement when greater clarity of truth is needed. I propose that with Integrative Science, that we create the same environment for spiritual evolution.

If you are a diligent, interested intellectual or scientific type and want to learn more, I direct you to Mill's book, _The Grand Unified Theory of Classical Quantum Mechanics_ or (CQM) (48). There is also an updated online version, copyright 2010, at BLPs website, which expands quite a bit on the original 2006 version that I cite here.

The BLP team has claimed to resolve both quantum level and macro level physics by a game changing assumption: The Schrödinger equation violates Maxwell's equations at the subatomic level. Therefore, Mill's group broke with QM traditional theory by using Maxwell's equations as a boundary condition for the Hydrogen atomic model. This novel model allows a more generalized form of hydrogen with possible the principle quantum number, n, to be either integers **AND** fractional numbers. The principle quantum number, n, classically describes the possible orbits of electron shells around the nucleus of an atom, which is taught in chemistry. Therefore Mill's model suggests that values of n can be the following: n {1, 2, 3 ...etc.} **AND** $1/n$ {½, 1/3, ¼, ... etc.}. Thus by questioning scientific dogma and resolving fundamental constituent equations at the subatomic, atomic, molecular, planetary and cosmic scales, the team has claimed to successfully integrate the great pillars of physics: quantum mechanics, electromagnetics (Maxwell's equations), Maxwell-Boltzmann molecular statistics, Gibb's thermodynamics, LaGrange's and Hamilton's elasticity and hydrodynamics, Gravity and special relativity, and Newtonian mechanics into the elusive Grand Unified Theory. Not only that, they also predict a *fifth fundamental force* based upon their calculations without relying on the fundamental assumptions that QM has been using for over 60 years.

Only repeatability, testing and time will tell if Mills and his team have revealed a new truth, but as you can see, the act of questioning fundamental assumptions is just as imperative to science as it is to spiritualism. I give kudos to any group that challenges the status quo for a noble purpose.

The reasons I include this particular group in the book are twofold. First, they have the courage and freedom to question scientific dogma, which has achieved almost a religious fervor. Second, they did not just look at theoretical or mathematical possibilities, which border on pure imagination in some cases, but they created a working generator technology that is being commercially licensed. Thirdly, they developed mathematical modeling software, based upon these assumptions, that correctly models a variety of organic molecules not achievable with previous methods, and produced experimental evidence from highly regarded independent parties.

Does that mean I believe everything the Mill's team proposes is truth? Not entirely. Why? Because, just like all humans, we perceive the world through assumptions taught to us or learned through experience. Many of these assumptions are flawed, and thus until we challenge them in a way to '*observe*' the flaw, they remain. Even with Mills group evidence against QM, there are probably hundreds of groups still reporting evidence in support of the theory. Perhaps Mill's work will turn the way of cold fusion. The jury is still out.

For instance, an article published in the 2008 issue of Nature, described an experiment than shows photon entanglement as a real measurable phenomenon. An example of photon entanglement is the ability of twin photons, created in the same instant, to continuously affect each other regardless of the distance between them, reportedly at faster than light speed. Salart and colleagues created twin photons and separated them via fiber optics by a distance of 18 km, thus each photon of the pair was literally in a separate town. They measured the photons properties which suggested that the photons were reacting to each other's measurements. This phenomenon is sometimes called 'spooky action at a distance'. For photons to react to each other at such a distance, the interaction between the two photons had to be at least 100,000 times the speed of light, which directly violates Einstein's theory of relativity. This result seems to challenge Einstein's assumption that all interactions between matter in the Universe is a locally causal phenomenon, meaning that the fastest interaction allowable would occur at the speed of light in a vacuum, c, or 3×10^8 m/s (49).

How is this possible? The result conflicts with Einstein's theory of special relativity, yet there it is. There is also proof of pulses of light traveling faster than the proposed speed of light in a dispersive dielectric (50). Perhaps the rules that govern physical causality are not the same rules that govern massless, nonphysical causality (such as information) as some have suggested (51), bringing us to a fundamental question of this discussion. Can interactions occur faster than light? If so, can information be exchanged faster than light and what does that imply for local causality, or local cause-and-effect interactions between mass particles that are limited by the speed of light. More importantly, does this explain or support spiritual existence? Before we can answer such questions, we need to dive deeper into the gap between cause-and-effect, the magical realm of the interaction.

THE REALM OF INTERACTIVE MAGIC:

*-Any aspect of reality, not entirely understood by logic,
experiment or science of the time, is aptly called Magic.-*

In the previous section we explored a multitude of theories about reality, so whose theory is right? It may be quite some time before science comes to some consensus on a single theory; however, regardless of what theory survives to win over the hearts and minds of humanity, these various theories all agree on one fundamental fact, humans interact with the Universe, at the physical and quantum levels. Furthermore, the fundamental disagreement appears to be over what speed the interactions occur, not whether or not they happen. Is there massless, information transfer? Absolutely, photons are massless quanta of energy that can carry information and have been used repeatedly using lasers and fiber optics. Can information transfer via entanglement or some other non-relativistic information theory? This is an area of heated research. If so, does it follow the same rules as our matter-energy based physics limited to the speed of light or do information theories rule? Is information matter, energy, negative-entropy or none of the above? Finally, from the spiritualism or humanistic perspective, do our conscious minds and intentions interact faster than light, governed by entanglement, or slower than light, governed by relativity, none of the above or all of the above?

Many shallow thinkers feel this line of questioning is silly, purely academic or even outrageous. However, in Noetic Science or the science of 'direct knowing', this line of questioning is taken very seriously. Experimental evidence suggests some people can draw or describe what another isolated subject is thinking, seeing or doing. According to, Dr. Marilyn Schlitz, President of the Institute for Noetic Sciences (IONS), scientists repeatedly find correlations of physiological influence of one subject on the other (52). To a physicist this may sound like a simple case of causality at work (not a disease). However, subjects are physically and more importantly <u>electromagnetically isolated</u> ruling out simple relativistic interactions such as photons or electromagnetic waves carrying information from the 'sender' to the 'receiver'. Thus, classical rules of physics fail to describe this type of information transfer and cannot even explain how it might be possible. In 2009, Radin and Borges published a research article, in the Journal Explore, titled *Intuition through time: what does the seer see?* They found that people could **anticipate** randomly distributed emotional photos evident in their unconscious pre-responses of spontaneous blinking and pupil dilation. In other words, people were exhibiting signs of emotional response to a randomly occurring photo, just prior to seeing it in time. Therefore, Radin and Borges suggest, the nature of intuition has some basis in the real world, effectively seeing into the immediate future (53). How is this possible? QM suggests entanglement theory which may be a possible conduit for information transfer outside of time, but perhaps, there are other explanations yet to be discovered. What they do know is that traditional, time-based cause-and-effect interaction is violated since the subject is somehow receiving the 'effect' before the 'cause' has even occurred in time. Perhaps this suggests another 'out-of-time' mechanism that we are unaware of.

Furthermore, Dr. Schlitz of IONS participated in an experiment many years prior designed to test if there is any correlation between high creativity and intuition. At Princeton, a collection of students from Julliard School of the Arts were chosen as isolated participants. The students participated as either a 'sender' or 'receiver' of random information presented to the sender alone. This repeatable 'Ganzfield' experiment places a 'receiver' in a dreamlike state, without actually being asleep. The 'receiver' has half 'ping-pong ball like' covers over their eyes while headphones play white noise in their ears to de-sense them from their immediate environment. In another isolated room, the 'sender' watched 1 of 4 randomly selected video clips that were themselves randomly selected from a collection of hundreds of clips. Dr. Schlitz was the 'sender' in some of these cases and recalls a scene from the movie Altered States in which the scene is bathed in red. Images of a crucifix appear then a coronal sun and finally a lizard opening and closing its mouth. She had headphones on listening to the other 'receiver' student in the 'ganzfield' state describing the crucifix the coronal sun and "red, red, red", and "I see a giant lizard opening and closing its mouth." Needless to say, it was her personal 'noetic' experience which propelled her into this unlikely career (52).

In an *EnlightenNext magazine* interview, Dr. Schlitz, goes on to say that after the experiment, the 'receiver' was allowed to look at all four video clips and choose which one matched what they 'saw'. Statistically, you have a 1 in 4 or 25% chance of correctly choosing. Interestingly, classically trained musicians had the greatest success rate at 75% of guessing the correct video clip, whereas the general Julliard population was about 50%, both well above statistical chance. The data is compelling and suggests that something profound is happening that we don't understand. All we know is, magic and mystery are alive and well within these interactions. Perhaps science will come up with some answers in the near future, but until then these interactions fall into the realm of mysticism and magic, simply because these expressions describe unknown or unexplainable events or occurrences by natural or logical means. A Zen viewpoint may yield the best insight:

There is no right. There is no wrong. There is only what is. What is measured and described changes.

Insight #10: We continuously interact with the Universe at multiple levels of scale via multiple mechanisms that are not entirely understood.

Are we are getting closer to understanding the Universe? Yes, in short. However, universal truth is an asymptote. Mathematically you can approach an asymptote but never actually reach it. Similarly, the closer we get to understanding the Universe, the smaller the knowledge gap. Paradoxically, the closer humanity gets the greater amount of energy and effort is required to obtain incremental answers.

Whether you subscribe to Quantum Theory, Classical Relativity or alternative Physics ideas, none of these models answer a fundamental question. Can there really be an 'objective observer' since all measurements and observations that we can conduct are also part of the Universe? If we are conscious beings that are made of the same matter and energy as that which we 'observe', then there really is just the change of the 'states' of matter at the Planck's scale within us as well, and thus no real separation or boundary of '*out there*' to '*in here*'. Scientifically speaking, we are truly products of star dust, supernovas and nebulae. Every subatomic particle and atom in our body, our literal mass-energy fabric, is as old as time; thus, *we are just as insignificant, and yet magnificent as the Universe itself.*

Insight #11: Nothing separates us from one another or the Cosmos, only the belief it is so.

The important underlying implications of quantum effects and change are humans. As conscious observers of the flow between states, we aid in the creation of reality as we know it, purely by the act of being present to realities unfolding. Absolute objectivity does not exist. Change is really the unseen interactions occurring between one moment to the next. This 'change gap' always underpins what will happen next and cannot be ignored or directly resisted. It would be like a flea standing against a Tsunami, sooner or later it will get swept along with the wave. We can; however, slightly influence the rules of the gap especially in large groups (45). After all, a single ant cannot survive seasons of weather, yet a colony can persist for years in all types of hostile environments. What scientific evidence has discovered is that **we definitely interact with our reality in measurable ways; furthermore, reality interacts with us.**

As far as we know, all things are composed of the same energy and matter (mass). Since energy can neither be created nor destroyed and mass is actually a form of bound energy, we also know that all energy and mass are continually interacting and continually transforming from one to the other (54) (55) (48). The nature of these interactions are mostly physically localized; however, entanglement theory hints that we may all be interacting globally as well (44) (45) (54) (49) (50). If that proves to be true, then every particle in your body has some entangled partner elsewhere in the Universe. As you affect the particles local to your direct sphere of influence (e.g. organisms you interact with, immediate surroundings, physical body, internal biochemistry, brain activity, thoughts and energy interactions) you are also affecting all of their entangled partners perhaps light years away via your intended and unintended actions.

CONSCIOUSNESS

-I am conscious of wind in my limbs and leaves, flashes of light and torrents of water pour over my trunk. Then an onrush of a persistent river surrounds me, tears at my roots, engulfs me to my most certain end. I awake again to being human.-

Consciousness is one of the most overused and misunderstood concepts in human language. A major source of this confusion is language itself. Physicist, Evan Harris Walker, author of *The Physics of Consciousness*, elegantly walks the fine line of physics, Zen philosophy and language to describe what consciousness is not. Walker's point is, to understanding consciousness one must first peel away what is not consciousness; what remains is then consciousness. Following this methodology we explore what consciousness is and its ramifications on our reality (44).

Consciousness is not *attention, focus* or *wakefulness* as many in the neuroscience or medical profession would have one believe.

Attention is where you are focusing your wakened mind and thus the three words above self-reference each other. Although these concepts play a role in consciousness, none of them apart or as a whole tell us what consciousness actually is. These are limiting human language terms. How do we know this? The simple case of dreaming defies medical definitions of consciousness. In a dream, who is experiencing the dream? Do you recall emotions, sensations, sights, sounds, tastes and smells of a dream? This is part of lucid dreaming and occurs mostly without external input to the mind. All humans and many animals have such repeatable experiences; however, medically speaking, they are all *unconscious*. Yet in the reality of the dream experience, we are aware of what was happening, can think and perceive, all of which are associated with conscious acts. Since consciousness is not adequately defined, we must dive deeper to uncover the definition of consciousness.

Instead let's try using analogies from Quantum Mechanics and Zen philosophy to tease out an answer, since we don't have an objective definition. QM suggests that it is not possible to obtain a true objective definition of events where the observer and observed are irreducibly coupled as is the case of consciousness and our individual minds. We cannot define objectively for example the *experience* of green. The experience of green for a blind person is not that of someone whose eyes are 'properly' converting light waves of a specific wavelength into neural impulses. However, even with sight, my experience of 'green' is uniquely different than your experience of 'green'.

The following are some meditative Zen style exercises to help you find the key to consciousness:

- Does a plant experience pleasure when the sun bathes it in warmth and light?

- How are you like the plant?

- Does a cup of water experience sorrow, loss or anxiety when separated from a water vapor?

- Since your body is mostly water, where is your body's evaporated water?

- Does an icicle experience pain when it breaks from an awning or when melting on the ground?

- What would you become if you were shattered into millions of pieces?

- Does an ant experience joy or pride when sharing with the colony that it found food?

- Are you the ant or the colony?

If you recognize that these questions are enthralling, expanding and sometimes dizzying, then you are starting to remove the veil covering consciousness. Consciousness is the center of all things, the interacting within the complex whole. Since we are only aware of changes or the transitions between moments, and at a fundamental level there is no definable separation between us and all things, *we only exist in the flow, in the gap, in consciousness*. Therefore universal consciousness is the flow everywhere, and human consciousness is but a small piece of that whole. For instance, you may have seen yourself experiencing the loss from the cup of water. It is because you created the cup from your own imagination and felt the loss of part of you in your mind. In reality, you never left the stream of consciousness. It is all around you. You are the stream, the ocean, consciousness; and consciousness is reality. The true path of enlightenment is revealed.

Insight #12: We are never separate from the flow of consciousness, or It us.

If you are beginning to fathom our discussions, we have unlocked the sphere of philosophy called Satori. Satori is a primary goal of Zen Buddhist philosophy and is experienced when a sudden enlightenment of consciousness is attained. The consciousness of consciousness, The Way, Zen, The Path, Enlightenment, Nirvana, all of these philosophical names from various traditions describe the same truth. Conscious enlightenment is not a destination, but a way of being in the stream of consciousness. On this path, there is no separation, no loneliness or loss, only understanding, accepting, experiencing and compassion.

The trick is not getting to a 'Satori', but staying in the flow of universal consciousness regardless of where you are, what you are doing and what is happening around you. If Zen Buddhist monks spend every minute of a lifetime or more mastering this, how can everyday people do it? Simple, the monks have no special key that you or I don't have; therefore nothing separates them from us. Thus, there is no particular formula that works best for everyone. You just need to practice using your key to unlocking the Universe every day. Practice viewing the Universe as it is, not as your ego or religion has made it out to be in your mind's eye.

FIELD CONSCIOUSNESS INTERACTIONS

N oetic science, psychological science and other disciplines have found that the more people align their intentions for a common outcome, the stronger the influence on the Universe and hence, reality (47). This phenomenon, called "Field Consciousness" has been extensively studied from small groups to millions and perhaps billions of people.

A basic experiment is as follows. A binary random number generator is an electronic device designed to create random distributions of '1s' or '0s'. Therefore, a perfect binary random number generator (RNG) would send out an equal amount of '1s' and '0s' for a given amount of time for a 50% probability of having either a '1' or a '0'. This is a robust statistical definition of randomness. The experiment begins by starting and acquiring data from one or more of these binary random number generator(s) to get a baseline level for randomness in an environment. If focused thought of an individual or group consciousness can affect outcomes in the Universe, effectively changing the probability from pure randomness to more order, then the RNGs should pick up this subtle change. In this case, more order would be significant deviation of the RNGs results away from 50/50 probability in the positive or negative direction; thereby creating favoritism for either the '1s' to come up or the '0s'. The RNG(s) are set to run before some event, run during the event and after the event to compare moments of intense interest to a baseline.

At first blush this idea may seem absurd, but take a moment to think about the implications of such a result. If it can be shown that either an individual or groups of individuals can affect a supposedly random outcome, then would it not be possible that anywhere and everywhere we collectively focus our attention or show great interest will have a measurable effect. Theoretically one or more intensely focused individuals could affect the level of order versus randomness in the Universe.

In fact, such experiments have been repeated multiple times with such implications resulting. For instance, Dr. Radin's group, formerly at the University of Nevada, Las Vegas (No surprise that the local Casino industry would have a vested interest in such research), ran a series of eight experiments which have shown that randomness is affected by local attention, global attention and focus, all aspects of the collective consciousness. The group sizes ranged from as small as 12 individuals in a personal growth intensive workshop, to approximately 200 million people watching and listening to Super bowl 1996 on up to an estimated 3 billion people watching the Opening Ceremonies of the July 1996 Olympic Games. **In all these cases, the period of time during the event, especially high interest moments, the RNGs deviated from pure random operation to a more ordered operation. In some cases the odds against random chance were as high as 1000 to 1** (45). The same RNGs showed very low deviation from randomness during control periods such as before and after the events.

Furthermore, the Princeton Engineering Anomalies Research (PEAR) program has been studying this phenomenon with smaller group sizes and individuals for over 30 years. The published evidence suggests that matter at many levels of scale is influenced by individual and group intention (46). In the PEAR's controversial book, *Margins of Reality*, by Robert Jahn and Brenda Dunne, the group suggests conventional sciences, in search of rigor and objectivity, has arbitrarily ignored the influences that human consciousness has on matter and reality.

> *Insight #13: The more you align yourself and others with divine flow the greater the influence either by intention, attention or entanglement.*

The question comes up, "Why then can I not just intend for something to happen to me and have it always happen?" Several answers have been suggested. Some say that the act of focused intention is very difficult to attain without rigorous training, such as, focus and meditative practices. Even then, we may not manifest everything we want. Others suggest that unless conscious entities' desires are aligned the responsive dynamics of the Universe are pulled in several conflicting directions with little to no net result.

The fundamental problem is that this line of thinking pulls our consciousness away from Universal consciousness. It does this because we focus on something specific that our ego desires not always what the soul or Source desires. Acting in a spiritually and consciously aligned way has the best chance of success because we are not trying to change the flow of the Universe, we are aligning with it. However, as the studies by PEAR and others suggest, human consciousnesses can create considerable effects when aligned together for common purposes, whether good or ill.

From these discussions, some questions arise in our mind. How and why can we, at human scale, affect electromagnetic systems, health, life, and quantum particles of the very fabric of the Universe? This leads to the study of another emerging branch of science, complexity.

CHAPTER 6
A COMPLEX
ADAPTIVE DANCE

-"I am because you are." –Ubuntu Philosophy

COMPLEXITY

-To understand complexity, you need to look no further than your body, a conscious collective of interacting agents-

It is well known that the human body is made up of several interworking systems, such as the cardiovascular system, the digestive system, the immune system and others. These systems provide certain functions for the whole organism to survive. Similarly, these systems are made up of organs that perform the various actions of the system, for instance the cardiovascular system includes the heart, arteries, veins, capillaries, and lymphatic vessels, which transport all of the nutrients to, and wastes from, the furthest reaches of the body. How is this system separable from you? It is not. Without all of the components, the system becomes incomplete and utterly shuts down, thus killing the whole organism.

This seems pretty obvious to an average person; however, we have only just begun to scratch the surface. The nutrients and gases are used by the collective workforce in the body, the cells. Cells are undeniably, with the unique DNA signature stamp, you. So much in fact, that your defense system, macrophages, Natural Killer (NK) cells, B and T-lymphocyte white blood cells and antibodies will search out and destroy any cell or organism that does not match what is uniquely your body. How do they know to do this? Why do they do this? Why does something microscopic in size sacrifice itself for me to be alive? The simple answer is our body as a whole would cease to exist and so the cells would die, but do the cells know this?

Higher education teaches the mechanisms of the molecules such as proteins, enzymes, DNA, RNA and extracellular matrix that allow for the cells to perform all of these amazing feats. Yet how do cells know their purpose in these activities? What goals do they have? Do cells have a mission or morality? This is a very Zen philosophy question that I ask my Anatomy and Physiology students. I typically get puzzled looks and few who dare to answer. Usually I get, after much contemplation, "well the cell is trying to stay alive..." If that were so, why would not all cells become like cancer cells and provide only for themselves for survival? More curious stares and thoughts usually come up with something like, "well cells need to work together to help each other stay alive..." and then a consensus from the class usually builds that goes along the simple lines of, "our body would cease to exist". Perhaps humanity as a whole could learn some lessons from our cells if we are to survive into the next century of our planet.

Going further down the rabbit whole, why do the molecules form the way they do? Why do enzymes, Nature's nano-machines, cut this or that protein apart or fuse amino acids or proteins together to make bones stronger or duplicate our genetic code? With all the expended biological energy, also known as adenosine triphosphate (ATP), why not take a vacation or a hiatus? Simply, if they did our body would cease to exist.

In Biochemistry, students learn that all life is based on chemistry. Ions, chemical reactions, Gibb's free energy and thermodynamics tell us that molecules move to ever greater states of entropy. If everything continuously moves toward more entropy, then how could we have started as two cells, the sperm and the egg, to become billions in a grand order of the human form? Why do the ions create action potentials in our muscles and neurons to allow us to move and think? Without these occurrences our body would surely never achieve existence in the first place.

To get answers, we dive deeper to the study of nuclear physics. Physicists have come to understand the inner workings of the atoms that make up these ions in search of truth. They learn about strong and weak forces, protons, neutrons and electrons, which loan or share themselves with other atoms in bonds to create grander structures. Nothing in your DNA molecule tells these electrons how to behave? Perhaps we bathe your body in ionizing X-ray radiation from an Image Guided Radiation Therapy (IGRT) machine to save your life from cancer. Are billions of electrons leaving your body replaced by others or simply lost? What then? Are you someone else or less of yourself? Have you gained or lost energy? These questions have no answers in traditional sciences, but they do have applicable meaning from the perspective of the spirit or soul. In fact most science completely ignores this observer existence perspective.

Deep in the rabbit hole, we rediscover the quantum level to explain such phenomenon and find that the rabbit hole is in fact circular, and takes us back to where we began with answers no more clear to us now then when we started. Humanity is just beginning to understand that this is a complex set of problems. However, answers may have been passing right in front of us all along yielding new types of systems study, the science of *Complexity*.

Look back at the previous paragraphs; notice anything interesting that happened as we moved down the scales of space and time? At different levels of scale, meaning size and duration in this case, we saw variations between order and disorder. For example, most of us agree that the human organism as a whole is less chaotic than say dust blowing in the wind. At this scale we appear as a distinct separate entity from other humans, animals, trees and rocks. Therefore, at this level of scale or size, we can easily perceive order from disorder, discriminate between objects and have adapted to identify patterns.

As we went to the systems level view of our body we again saw emergent forms of organs combining together to create a system, our body. I can differentiate the heart from the artery, but they are distinctly inseparable functionally. If I do, I break down the subsystem of either or the whole and the body in which it supports.

The organs are discrete forms that arise from their constituent cells, which reveal chaotic to orderly tissue organization. Under the microscope, science again discovers order from chaos when looking at the cells themselves and finds they too have organ like systems called organelles.

Science has continued the search for this hidden order using macromolecular crystallography technology to view things at the nano-scale. Here scientists discover that molecular order dominates this landscape, even though looking at the collective interactions of molecules from a slightly larger scale appears chaotic.

At the level of atoms using Atom Force Microscopy (AFM), scientists can literally 'see' sphere like structures of various diameters related to the element type. Again, order emerges from apparent disorder.

Subatomic particles are no exception; however, our ability to measure such things is limited. Subatomic particles are measured by their interactions when physicists crash them together at speeds close to the speed of light. Once again, mathematical equations and graphical models yield order from the chaos of quarks and probabilistic uncertainty. Protons can be shown to have a radius, electrons a mass and its anti-matter mirror image, the positron, a positive charge (48) (56).

So what are we to make of all these discoveries? Apparent order seems to self-appear at various levels of scale, but how? We don't have a computer fast enough or with enough memory to compute all of the first principle mathematics to answer these questions, *or* do we? Technology advances in computational science have shown us some interesting shortcuts, revealing insights to complex systems when complete computation would have been nearly impossible.

Before we go too far into this discussion, let's clarify the scope and meaning of complexity science. Observation, study and modeling emergent order and behavior from complex adaptive systems (CAS) are the heart of complexity science. Figure 4 below shows a modified diagram of emergent order from seaming chaos at the individual agent level. This diagram is based upon Chris Langdon's original ideas and diagrams at the Santa Fe Institute (57). The graphical representation of emergent behavior arises from various rules that each of the interacting agents follow. At the level of interacting agents, represented as various shapes with arrows of informational, energetic or material exchange, the agents possess adaptability characteristics (rule sets), or ways the agents can modify their behavior with respect to their internal and external environment. As each interaction occurs between agents, each involved agent uniquely interprets the interaction and responds differently depending upon its internal rule set and the external environment. These agents represent discrete individual players contributing to a collective system based upon some observable or definable rules.

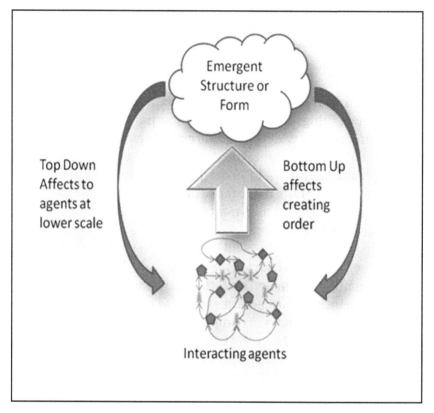

Figure 4: Graphical representation of the property of emergence (order) at the top from seemingly chaos (disorder) at the bottom for different orders of scale.

Real world examples of agents are quantum particles, atoms, molecules, cells, humans, investors, soldiers, ships, money, bees, ants and trees, on up to planets, stars and galaxies. For instance, a cell adapts to its changing environment by expressing different proteins. Most people recognize that individuals adapt their social behavior to external pressures from friends, colleagues or managers. Do you behave the same way in front of close friends as you do your boss? Ultimately if we pull our focus back up the scale of the collective behavior, we see an emergent behavior or structure of the system that appears very orderly even when the underlying agent interactions appear chaotic.

Such examples of large scale emergent structures or behaviors are organisms, bee hives, countries, democracies, capitalism, religion, Earth, stars or galaxies. Note that some of these emergent systems are, in fact, agents of a larger system as well. This is well understood in the complexity science field which begs the question, "what is the largest complex adaptive system known to man?" The answer is the entire Universe. Outside of the known Universe, there is speculation that it may interact with other Universes, but it is still yet unproven.

There has been an explosion of research in the past decade and rise of strategy consulting firms using complexity science combined with computation to model and advise on everything from economic forecasting for traders and investment banks to global climate change. What is novel in this model from older ones is that many emergent systems also transfer information back down to the scale of the agents; thus further modifying their behavior and the behavior of the system as a whole. Rather than explain another example, I would rather you prove it to yourself with a little, 'noetic'/physiologic experiment.

Thought Exercise:

1. Take a moment alone and find a quiet place to comfortably stand.
2. Pay close attention to your heart beat or your pulse. Note your pulse rate in beats/minute.
3. Now choose to sit and relax for one minute.
4. Observe what happens to your heart rate again.
5. Now choose to focus on your breathing.
6. Breathe slow deep controlled inhalations and long relaxed exhalations. Slow your breathing down from ~12 breaths per minute to 6 or 7 breaths per minute.
7. Once you have done so or if you are close, take note of what has happened to your heart rate.
8. Has it increased or decreased.

9. Ask yourself this question, "Did your cells (agents) cause that change in you or did you (emergent structure) choose, of your own volition, the change and your cells followed?

Who did the choosing? Was it some random firing events of neurons in your brain that dictated to your body what needed to happen or did some emergent collective entity, you in this case, do it? What is this emergent entity? Is it your body, your mind, your soul? Where is the identity, the observer, 'you'? What are 'you'? For that matter what does that make 'us' or 'we'?

HOW DOES ORDER EMERGE FROM CHAOS?

-Chaos inhales life into Order. Order exhales life into Chaos.-

In order to better understand complexity, the science of order from chaos, and how it affects us directly, we need to understand what order and chaos actually mean. Stephen Wolfram, a mentor of mine, wrote a seminal paper on system behavior, revised in his treatise titled, *A New Kind of Science* or (NKS) for short. I was very fortunate when NKS was published, to participate in the first NKS class in 2003 to study these issues with Wolfram in a summer retreat at Brown University. In 2004, many of us presented our work at the 1st Annual New Kind of Science Conference.

In NKS, four classes of behavior are defined. A simple demonstration of the four classes is digitally simulated via interacting rules for binary or grayscale pixels to evolve structure in what is called cellular automata or (CA) (58). Wolfram was able to demonstrate four emergent behaviors even with the simplest of binary systems. An initial condition and a single point were defined. Then an 8 bit binary rule set, pictured in Figure 5, was then identified by a unique decimal number between 0-255. The rules completely determine the transition of each *iteration* or step. Each step can represent a step in time or space with regard to agent interactions. Wolfram further classified the four behaviors, shown in Figure 5 below, as; Class I) Simple, Class II) Simple-Repeating, Class III) Random and Class IV) Complex.

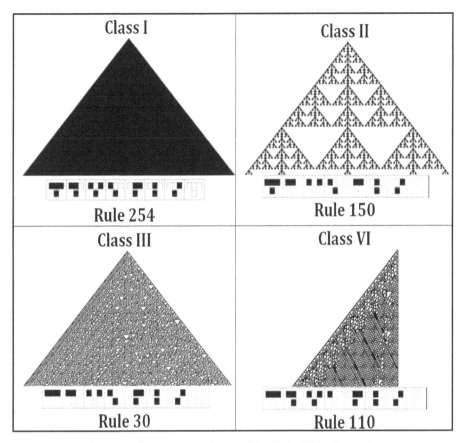

Figure 5: Class I behavior is depicted by Rule 254 where the system behavior goes to a steady state of all black. Notice the Rule name, 254 in this case, is the decimal number that represents the binary rule set containing 8 possible scenarios that internally 'decide' whether the next point should be white or black. Class II behavior shown by Rule 150 shows a nested triangle pattern. Class III behavior shown by Rule 30 shows a random behavior, which was further proven to be a robust random number generator. Class IV shown by Rule 110 shows only half of the triangle to emphasize the portion showing complex behavior that is not repeated, even when run for millions of iterations. (Courtesy of Mathematical Explore software)

Class I behavior is a system that follows a basic rule set and eventually collapses to a single outcome or state. This is analogous to a pendulum of a grandfather clock that will swing back and forth, but with loss of energy due to friction, will ultimately stop to a fixed state at the bottom of the arc.

Class II behavior depicted in Figure 5 shows the system following a different rule set yet has obvious repeatability or periodicity with respect to the structures in the system. There are simple versions of Class II behavior such as a checkerboard pattern. However, Rule 150 shows a more interesting nested pattern or fractal, which means it displays repeating pattern characteristics at many levels of scale. We will discuss fractals in more detail later. The triangle is a common shape among mathematics and modern works of art (58).

Class III behavior shown in Figure 5 is a system following yet another rule option, Rule 30. This system appears to have random structure size and order, and in fact, was proven to be a better random number generator than most previous random number generation algorithms. I must confess when I first saw Rule 30; I did not quite understand that I was looking at a random number generator. Then I considered that it began with a specific initial condition and the randomness was generated during each iteration. If you start with a random initial condition, the system appears more uniformly random. If you are interested in learning more, I urge you to read the section on randomness in NKS (58).

Finally, Class IV behavior depicted in Figure 5 represents complex behavior. Wolfram defines complex behavior as lying somewhere in between purely random, like the Class III system, and purely ordered as in the Class I or II systems. Furthermore, Wolfram postulates that Class IV systems may all be capable of *universal computation*. In a nutshell, universal computation is a system that has the ability to model or compute any other system. Many systems are universal computational systems similar to Rule 110, such as the Turing machine. The Turing machine is named after Alan Turing, whose research work formed the foundations of modern computers and computing. We will revisit universal computation and its implications on spiritual theory in a later section.

You may be thinking, 'That is great, but what does this have to do with the real world?' If you have followed the conversation thus far, it means a great deal. All things, including computer simulations, are linked at the quantum level. The digital world is still governed by the same underpinning universal laws and therefore fundamentally a subset of reality as a whole.

It turns out that the engineering world, in which the depth of my training is in, has similar classifications for real world systems on the scales that engineers have to deal with all the time in design. Particularly if engineers want to design a dynamic system, such as a robot, rocket, chemical processing machine, pacemaker or even an intelligent prosthetic to help an above the knee amputee to walk again, they need to come up with some type of controllable behavior. The analogy that we see in these simulated systems is that we are looking at the binary equivalent of what engineers and scientists see in higher level real systems, except we classify them using engineering and scientific terms for the same phenomenon.

To map Wolfram's digital classifications to engineering dynamics language, we have:

- Class I → Static

- Class II → Periodic

- Class III → Pure Randomness (a.k.a. White Noise)

- Class IV → Complex or Chaotic.

Using these engineering terms, we can now talk about real system behavior that you or I can visualize or see every day.

Static system behavior is probably the least interesting since, as its name implies, it is eventually not in motion or changing. A typical example is a building, a ball lying at the bottom of a bowl or my children when I first ask them to clean their rooms (well perhaps not the last one). This is a scale dependent classification, because in a complex world, even a model of a static system has non-static components at smaller levels of scale.

Periodic system behavior is characterized by a repeating pattern that transforms motion to potential energy and back again. The swinging pendulum of a grandfather clock, the spin of a bicycle tire and the rotation of a Ferris wheel are all examples of periodic systems. Unlike the static system above, the periodic system will stay in motion as long as a little bit of energy is added to the system to offset energy losses from the system.

A random system behaves statistically similar to Wolfram's simulation above where the outcomes or *information content* is infinite and incompressible. Thus a random systems behavior is truly unpredictable. In other words, if we try to compress a purely random set of numbers using a compression program (algorithm), such as the MP-3 or Advanced Audio Coding (AAC), part of the MP-4 compression specification that iPods use, we could not shrink the file size (59). A more tangible, real world example is white noise appearing as 'white snow' on analog TV channels that have no broadcast. Modern Digital Televisions (DTV) scan for channel signals and skip the others. The analog TVs show all possible channels (frequency bands) that it could tune to, so white random noise was easily found. A more technical definition of white noise is a uniform (equal) power distribution across all frequencies, meaning that the noise is spread evenly from 0Hz to infinity. It turns out that this white background noise is believed by most physicists to be the microwave background of the entire Universe dating back to the beginning.

The fourth and final system is the Complex or Chaotic system, which is literally the fuzzy border between pure randomness and periodicity. This is the realm of Chaos and is arguably the most interesting system. Complexity and chaos is where life exists. Many science disciplines have emerged to study these systems; such as Chaos Theory, Fractals, Cellular Automata, Complexity Science, Complex Adaptive Systems, Network Dynamics, Systems Biology, Integrative Systems, Multi-input Multi-output (MIMO) Feedback Systems, Multi-nonlinear System Analysis, Artificial Intelligence, New Kind of Science and Emergence Theory.

All of these fields have some relationship to each other and have vast numbers of brilliant scientists exploring the edge of dynamic beauty and intrigue. See the *Works Cited* section for some selective introductory books on many of these topics (57) (60) (61) (62) (57) (63). Rather than try to reproduce the definitions and studies in all of these disciplines, I will highlight the discoveries that have profound implications to our everyday life and our spiritual existence.

THE EDGE OF CHAOS

We exist in a complex world and therefore fall into the Class IV system. Because this system is complex, it has fuzzy, hard to define edges. The only mathematical concept that best describes such a boundless border comes from Chaos theory. Before we go too far; however, we must agree to a definition of Chaos, since Chaos in the scientific terminology is quite different than that of common language.

In the pre-Socratic era, during the time of Hesiod, the word χάος (Khaos) represented the moving, formless void, or 'primordial, non-being state' from which the cosmos and gods, Gaia, Tartarus, Erebus, Nyx and Eros originated (64). In earlier cultures, Chaoskampf represented the conflict between order and randomness commonly represented by mythical characters depending upon culture, pantheon and period. Marduk, representing order, fought Tiamat, the agent of chaos, in the Babylonian Enuma Elish myths. Baal battled Yamm in Ugaritic mythology. Yahweh faced Leviathan in the Hebrew mythology. Thor continuously tried to defeat the Midgar serpent in Norse mythology (65). All of these mythological themes represent order versus disorder. Even Christianity borrowed the same themes creating St. George versus the Dragon and St. Michael versus the Devil (66). Historically, the struggle of humanity trying to bring about order and stability to their world has always led to conflict with the chaotic and unstable forces of nature giving rise to mythological explanations (67). It was not until Elizabethan times and the modern English language did the term Chaos take on the current meaning of complete disorder and confusion; however, as we have seen, this is quite a deviation from its origins.

When I use the term Chaos in this book, I am referring to the science of Chaos and associated Chaos Theory that has emerged. Specifically, a chaotic system has an infinite fractal border with pseudo-periodic behavior that is self similar, but never exactly repeats. What is a fractal? A fractal has a unique characteristic. If one zooms in on any portion of its boarder, more detail reveals itself with a similar, yet not exact, pattern as other levels of scale. We can see fractal images in Figure 6, the most famous example of chaotic structure called the Mandelbrot Set, discovered by Benoit Mandelbrot (1924-2010) for whom it is named.

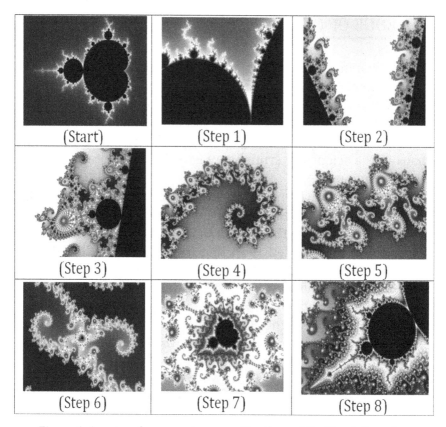

(Start)	(Step 1)	(Step 2)
(Step 3)	(Step 4)	(Step 5)
(Step 6)	(Step 7)	(Step 8)

Figure 6: A series of progressive magnifications of the Mandelbrot Set. Notice how a variation of the original set reemerges in Step 7. (Free use License by GNU licensing via Wikimedia)

This amazing chaotic system, with fractal borders, is created from solving a simple iterative equation, $Z_{i+1} = (Z_i)^2 + C$, for a set of complex numbers. For those not familiar, a complex number has two parts to it, a real part, R, and an imaginary part, I, which is strictly multiplied by 'i', a simple place holder for the value square root of -1. The reason for the 'i' placeholder is that the square root of -1 has no valid answer by itself without help, such as being multiplied by itself an even number of times (e.g. $i^2 = -1$, $i^3 = -i$, $i^4 = 1$, etc.). Thus an example of a complex number is written as 3 + 2i. On a complex plot, the X-axis represents the real number component plotted against the Y-axis the imaginary number components. Therefore to plot a complex number is the same as plotting a coordinate pair in algebra. For example, to plot 3 + 2i we count 3 positive spaces to the right on the x-axis and 2 positive spaces up on the y-axis and place our dot on the graph like Figure 7.

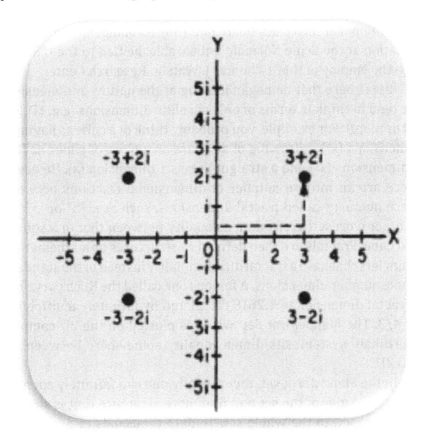

Figure 7: Plot of 3+2i. Also shown is -3+2i; -3-2i and 3-2i.

This is the same coordinate system used to test if points are in the Mandelbrot Set or not. Take a point, say 3 +2i, plug it into the iterative Mandelbrot equation for C and $Z_0=0$ and solve for Z_{i+1}. Every solution gets plugged back into Z_i for each successive calculation. If the equation converges to an answer within so many iterations, then it is part of the Mandelbrot Set and is colored black. If the equation does not converge to a number, but instead diverges, the point is colored based upon how fast the point diverges and voila!

Benoit Mandelbrot, the man, is equally fascinating. By separating from orthodox approaches to mathematics imposed on students by the prestigious French institutions; École Normale and École

Polytechnique, Mandelbrot was a bit of a mathematical maverick. Benoit found that he was adept at finding geometrical solutions to solving mathematical problems which was frowned upon by conventional French mathematicians (60). As Mandelbrot found the situation at the École Normale unbearable, he fled to the U.S. and into the employ of IBM's Thomas J. Watson Research Center.

It was here that he began looking at the nature of dimension. We tend to think in terms of only absolute dimensions (e.g. 1D, 2D, 3D or more). For example, you probably think of a cube as having 3 dimensions (x^3), a drawing of a square on a piece of paper having 2 dimensions (x^2) and a straight line as 1 dimension (x). However, there are an infinite number of dimensional fractions between these numbers called fractal dimensions, such as $x^{1.2456}$ or $x^{2.66743}$. In other words, there is dimensionality between that of a square and cube. Fractals are then defined as structures or mathematical behaviors that have a fractal dimensionality instead of the standard whole number dimensions. A famous one called the Koch curve has a fractal dimension of 1.2618 calculated by infinitely multiplying by 4/3. The Mandelbrot Set, which is plotted on the 2D complex coordinate system, sits dimensionality somewhere between 1D and 2D.

In the Mandelbrot set, theoretically one can infinitely zoom in on any boarder of the set and find more structure that is similar, yet not exact, to the whole set. To date thousands of people and automated computers have tried debunking this assumption, but none have succeeded (60). Furthermore the Mandelbrot set is considered the 'Master Set' of all fractal sets, because all other mathematical fractal sets, called Julia Sets, are found within the infinite border.

In real life, how do we see fractal structures? The repeating patterns in fronds of a fern, leaves of a tree or branches of a bush are all fractal patterns. Coastlines of land masses are global examples where fractal structures are 'self-similar'. This can be easily demonstrated by using Google Earth to look at a coastline anywhere in the world. Zoom in as many times as possible and what do you notice? The coastline presents a very similar pattern at various levels of scale. If fractal structures appear everywhere in nature, we could postulate that all complex structures have some level of fractal character. If that is true, and we perceive the human brain and integrated neural system as structurally complex creating a modified neural network, it follows that at other levels of scale there ought to be complex networks at larger and smaller levels of scale. Furthermore, if the human mind is seated in the structure of our bodies, what is seated in the complex network structure of the Universe? A Universal Mind? If so, is this the body of the Source we have been searching for? It is a tantalizing proposition which requires additional evidential support.

Chaos is similar to fractal structures except that it describes system behavior instead of structure. Chaotic systems also have complex, yet similar dynamic behavior that never exactly matches previous behavior. In short chaotic systems are the dynamic equivalents of fractals. The most obvious example is global weather patterns, which have seasonal similarities, yet are never exactly the same. The annual publication of the *Farmer's Almanac* was famous for this very reason. Farmers understand that the seasons are mostly cyclical, key word 'mostly'. They also wanted to see the larger trends for several years to try to predict for droughts and wet seasons, so they could better plan their crops.

The classic mathematical example comes from Edward Lorenz (1917-2008) who ironically studied weather patterns and accidently came across a chaotic system that has been aptly named the Lorenz Attractor. Much has been written about this system, but the key is that it comes from equations describing the behavior of fluids. The Lorenz Attractor has been exhaustively studied and shown to be continuously chaotic with a fractal dimension of 2.06 +/- 0.01. These results essentially mean that chaotic system behavior *is* related to fractal patterns with infinite boarders (60).

I suspect all three dimensional chaotic systems may be fractals between the third and fourth dimension if we define the fourth dimension as time instead of the traditional space. More formalized work is being done to confirm or refute this idea, but it makes logical sense. Since these chaotic systems have infinite boarders as their fractal cousins, what does this infinite edge of chaos physically mean to us?

I remember the first time, studying the Mandelbrot Set in graduate school. We had formed a small collective group loosely called, the Complexity Group, in the Bioengineering department at Arizona State University, which was dedicated to studying complexity as it applied to biological and engineered systems. We later formalized the discussions into a one hour exploratory course for other students; however, most of us participated for the shear fascination, not the credits. It became apparent as we opened our minds to this realm of science; we had no idea where it would lead us. More importantly, once our eyes opened to what was happening all around us, we could never again return to our former blindness. At this point we saw fractal patterns and chaotic behavior everywhere we looked at multiple levels of scale. It became readily apparent to me then that the relationship between reality and mathematics was simultaneously profound and subtle. If these connections of complexity and chaos are part of the world around us and within us, then would that not also include our minds and perhaps our spirit? I needed to understand more, and the engineer in me, needed a concrete bridge to the engineering sciences.

The Mandelbrot Set looked strikingly similar to systems that I, as an engineer, designed every day to control systems. I had created control systems for incubator temperatures, dynamic microfluidic flow systems, robotic arms, DOD test systems, heart and brainwave monitoring systems and prosthetics. Engineers call these relatively simple control systems *Feedback Control Systems*. A plot commonly used to tell how a system performs is called the Nyquist Diagram (See Figure 8), which interestingly is plotted in the same complex coordinate system as the Mandelbrot Set. Notice how the simple controllable engineering system's geometry is a gross simplification of the Mandelbrot Set. Do the similarities suggest that there is a link between physical systems and the iterative complex mathematics that we see with the Mandelbrot Set?

Therefore, in the real and mathematical worlds, complex behavior arises under the right conditions.Due to this fact, the following hypothesis may be posed: *The edge of Chaos represents a border through which deterministic systems are perturbed by outside information from the rest of the Universe.* What does this statement mean in practical terms? These universal interactions occur in every system within the known Universe. Thus, there is continuous information transfer (e.g. physical perturbations, noise, entanglements and interactions) with all systems at multiple levels of scale throughout the cosmos. It does not matter whether the system is an intermittently stable atom, a simple household thermostat or a chaotically stable human heart. Perhaps the Mandelbrot Set represents of this edge of Chaos. It may very well be a mathematical snapshot of universal entanglement revealing an infinite window through which information transfers at all levels of scale simultaneously.

Insight #14: The complex dance of Life and Universe, as an integrated whole, is eternally played out between order and disorder revealing a divine unfolding.

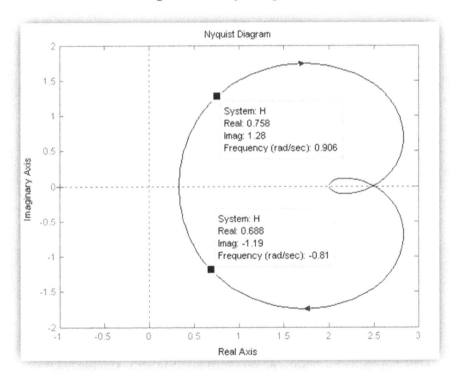

Figure 8: Example Nyquist plot of a stable 2nd Order feedback control system showing the same symmetry along the x-axis, real numbers that the Mandelbrot Set shows. (Used with permission by GNU free license, author Benjamin Bradu PhD, Université Paris-Sud 11 and CERN, from http://fr.wikipedia.org/wiki/Fichier:Diag_nyquist.JPG accessed Aug. 17, 2010.)

COMPLEX INTERACTIONS ON THE EDGE

It is a bit dizzying contemplating an infinite boarder, but that is the realm where Nature exists and complex adaptive systems (CAS) play. In the previous complexity section, we introduced CAS, which exhibits both order (stable) and chaos (random) behavior to form emergent structures at larger levels of scale (Refer to Figure 4 in the Complexity section).

Let's dive a bit deeper into CAS to better understand what they are and how they apply to the subject of spirituality. In order to do so we need to define some of the terms so there is no confusion in the translation. John Holland, one of the early pioneers of genetic algorithms has written extensively on CAS and provides a great introduction to the terminology I will be using here. For those who are interested on such topics, I suggest reading Holland's books; *Hidden Order: How Adaptation Builds Complexity* and *Emergence: From Chaos to Order* (62) (61).

As you may recall, CAS are made up of independently interacting agents. An agent is a self contained unit in a group of agents that follows various rules. To elaborate, visualize a bird (agent) in a flock (aggregate agent). The bird (agent) has some general rules while flying like:

1. Do not get to close to another bird
2. Do not fly away too far from flock
3. Land when other birds do; and so on.

Notice the bird is an adapting piece of the whole flock. The whole flock follows its own collective behavior which emerges from these internal interactions of the birds. There are also unforeseen external interactions that can affect the flock, such as a car speeding toward the flock on the highway or a predator jumping out near the flocks landing site. These events will quickly alter the entire flock behavior to minimize the threat to the flock and subsequently the individual birds; however, often a single bird may be sacrificed to preserve the flock. In this way we see what was evident in nature; a group behaves simultaneously as a whole entity and as a group of individuals. Is society any different? Economies? What about the entire planet?

The key feature of all CAS is *adaptation*. Adaptation is defined as the ability to modify behavior or rules within an agent. In our last example, the bird and the flock had to adapt when the car drove into their path. Adaptation occurs on a timescale appropriate to the system. For example the human central nervous system (CNS) modifies its rules approximately within a timeframe of milliseconds to hours; whereas, our immune system's behavior will take hours to days to modify its rules and adapt to new perturbations, such as a viral infection. A business can take months to years to modify its behavior, and species days to centuries depending upon the level of adaptation required. A continuous stream of adaptation that leads to survival in a species is what we call evolution. If the cumulative adaptations are distinct enough from the previous species, we classify it as a new species and we say the species "evolved". However, there is an ongoing debate as to what level of change is required to classify a new species.

Thought experiment:

If we define the progression of all life in terms of adaptation and dispense with the notion of evolutionary classifications, how does that change our perception of our relationship to Australopithecines? Mammals? Dinosaurs? Plants? Bacterium? Viruses? Atoms? Photons?

The key point of CAS is that the individual agents interact with each other and their environment with adaptable and optimizable rules, which ultimately generates emergent behavior and larger scales of order, we recognize as objects. Again, our body is a great example of what is meant by emergence. But we don't stop with our own body as an emergent entity of the collective cells within. People are agents of collective social entities as well. We even have conventional names for the small scale entities like schools, companies, churches and others. If we include all of the interacting agents, such as, soil, plants, trees, animals, natural resources, land features, chemicals, gases and so on, we can classify larger entities such as towns, cities, states, provinces, countries and ultimately the global dynamic community, Earth. We suddenly become aware of an expansive notion: ***There is no limit to the system scope. No boundary of complexity or size that we can distinctively draw. It simply continues through the Universal scale.***

Granted, this realization can be quite overwhelming and fantastically beautiful at the same time. Humanity is increasingly using tools, computer programs and object oriented algorithms to model and understand these complex systems. A recreational example that you have probably played or heard of is the computer game called The SIMS™. This program and others like it are based upon interactive agents (SIM Characters) who modify their behavior as the game is played by responding to interactions with other characters and circumstances. Furthermore, modern weather, global warming, the economy, warfare and supply chain management models are all applications of the complex adaptive system approach.

The advent of computer processing power has enabled us to plow the fields of complexity reaping numerous research projects going into the foreseeable future. What does all of this modeling mean to the average person and what is it all for? The goal for most of these artificial CAS is to create a model of a real world CAS, allowing us to make predictions about real systems that surround us every day. Computational Science has proven that simpler systems with few rule sets can predict behavior to a limited extent. However, any complex system yields less predictable results the further out in time (or in computational speak, iterations) that you try to predict.

Limited predictability is the same phenomenon Lorenz saw in weather models. We can only predict with some statistical certainty for about a day or so and after that it is anybody's guess even for expert meteorologists. There is a common joke that if meteorologists are right 40% of the time with their weather predictions, then perhaps they should just say the opposite of what their models tell them so they can be right 60% of the time. If it were that simple, I am sure a meteorologist would be doing it already. Humor aside, the joke also underlies common misunderstandings that the common populace has with complex system predictions. The uncertainty of weather prediction is due in part to what Lorenz called the 'butterfly effect' (60). A butterfly flaps its wings in Singapore and the cascading set of causal events culminate for the right conditions to create a hurricane in Texas; chaos plays its role. The chaos effect, interacting at multiple levels of scale, constantly moves future weather outcomes by the most subtle means.

From a spiritual perspective, if even the smallest events can have a dramatic effect on our lives, what does that suggest about the power of our thoughts and intentions? Mountains of evidence show that thoughts and intentions have a subtle effect on the environment around us (45). A particularly interesting one is a double blind study on the effects of remote positive intentions on water crystallization formation. In this study, 2000 people in Japan focused positive intentions on electromagnetically isolated water samples in California. The participants were unaware of a control set samples that were used as a comparison. Then randomized photographs of the water crystallization were taken and 100 volunteers from the internet were asked to rate each crystal's aesthetic quality on a scale from 0 (not beautiful) to 6 (very beautiful). The data shows that the water crystals that were "treated" with pleasant intentions had a significantly higher (P<0.001) aesthetic appeal score than that of the control water crystals. This result reinforces two theories; 1) Thoughts and Intentions affect the material world around us and 2) That effect is not communicated via classical physics (i.e. light or other electromagnetic radiation) (68). If this is true, according to Chaos Theory, a well timed and placed thought, intention or act can be highly amplified by natural complex interactions (60) (57). What then is the potential for small acts of kindness and compassion for the global landscape? What are the potential consequences for small acts of prejudice, hate or dispassion? If a butterfly can catalyze a hurricane, what is the power of expressing compassion to your fellow man or the environment? Take some time to answer these questions in your mind. How do these answers affect our tremendous responsibility in this world? Just exercising a little logic reveals how local actions and decisions, moral or immoral, cascade into a global reaction. *The actions of the one do indeed affect the many.*

Much to the frustration of many engineers, a natural system with so many variables does not lend itself to traditional control methods. This should not be a surprise. Just try controlling the flow of water in a bathtub with your hand. Several unintended patterns emerge and the water develops eddies or becomes turbulent. However, modern control theory has found a new method to control systems using **chaotic control** algorithms. For example, a group of engineers at NASA were able to efficiently control a satellite using a chaotic control method. The method essentially nudges the satellite at the exact right times to adjust the trajectory using a minimal amount of fuel (69). Despite these new paradigms, we still tend to simplify, simplify, simplify to get anything man made to work in the context of such complex surroundings.

Knowing now that we are inseparable from the complex system in which we find ourselves physically, mentally, spiritually and informationally immersed, somehow nature found a way for our bodies to sustain relative stability for a period of time. Many scientists and engineers are in awe of this fact. We try to understand the simplest of systems in the human body and quickly get overwhelmed by the complexity of feedback control responses interacting at multiple levels of scale. The human body, and by extension all living organisms are truly miraculous.

Expanding our thinking, we find that all life finds a niche within this global complex adaptive system we call Earth. Our planet constantly balances gases, liquids and solids in the biosphere. What becomes evident is that Earth's chaotic balance I not unlike our own body. More importantly, Earth's balancing act is also created by living and non-living agents, similar to all living organisms. This revelation gave rise to the Gaia theory interpretation-- that the Earth is a living entity with all the complexities of life (70). I submit a modified interpretation that Gaia (Earth) not only is a living system, but it is an evolving organism (i.e. developing its subsystem equivalents of organelles or organs). Before humans, the planet predominantly transferred or received information via naturally occurring pathways such as weather, air, liquids and solids. Sunlight is the external energy source feeding the planet. Human's have accelerated Earth's development by adding effective informational and energetic networks via satellites, wireless, electrical and fiber optic cables. Perhaps this may be the dawn of the new Earth Mind. It is increasingly apparent that for us to spiritually evolve we need to change our perspective of what our individual purpose and role is here and what humanity really is in the grander scheme.

> **Insight #15: All naturally occurring complex adaptive systems, and by implication all Life, simultaneously emerge from smaller agents of scale and contribute to a larger emergent being as agents.**

UNIVERSAL COMPUTATION AND INFORMATION FLOW

-Those listening to the Source of flow are informed; those constantly speaking miss the information and are thus misinformed-

We come to an intersection of sciences. Complex systems, such as humans, cats, dogs, and much of life behave as Class IV living systems. However, what does this imply? Class IV living systems have the interesting and possibly unique ability to model the world around them, make decisions and act on those decisions.

A fairly common occurrence in Arizona is a dog will see a rattle snake and instinctively want to sniff it. Barring that no malevolent consequence of sniffing a snake has ever occurred with this dog, it will probably sniff the snake, get bit and need to be rushed to the Vet for a shot of anti-venom.

Let's take our loyal dog, and add the element of learned pain or fear (adaptation) from the dog's last experience to the equation. The dog again sees a rattle snake. The dog learned (unless they are a very slow learner) from their last mistake, project in their mind what may happen if they sniff the snake and avoid the event all together by backing away. In fact, this is not a hypothetical situation, in Phoenix where I currently live; there are snake trainers for hire that will train dogs how to avoid rattle snake bites. The trainer uses a defanged rattle snake that will instinctively defend itself from the curious canine. This 'scare tactic' safely and effectively trains the dog to back away and avoid the snake.

Thus, a complex adaptive system, the dog, processes the event into memory (acquiring input data), computationally creates a model of what may happen for a similar event (prediction), adjusts its internal rules from sniff to back up (adaptation) and executes the new action (decision) based upon what was learned. This process is an incredible computational feat by modern standards and should not be taken lightly. Computer programmers would have had to encode thousands of lines of code to achieve this single act of the dog using traditional algorithms.

Complex adaptive systems combined with fuzzy logic rules and learning neural networks are able to approach this behavior and in fact, *computationally speaking* are closer approximations to how our minds operate. I highlight *computationally speaking* because I don't suggest that we are just a computer program, we are much more. The idea is to distinguish what is computation in terms of reality and what does this exchange of information mean to us.

Computation is by definition that act or action of computing or calculating according to Merriam-Webster's online dictionary. Although technically correct in its simplicity, the definition only describes part of the story. Computation in the modern world usually implies the use of a computational device such as a computer, calculator, or application on a cell phone or iPad. The variations are vast, yet even this does not cover all the bases. The act of computation can be performed by *anything* capable of performing computation.

What do I mean by that? In general, anything can receive input information and return some output computed from that input. Engineers like to call this the 'black box'; some input goes in, gets modified and the output comes out. Computation does not require electronics nor does it need to be particularly advanced. For example, I push on a pedal attached to the sprocket on my bicycle at a particular speed and force. My bike internalizes the input (pedals transmit my effort), magnifies my effort through a chain connected to the back wheel sprocket of specific radius (computes) and propels me forward (outputs result).

A much more sophisticated example is the ant body and nervous system. Visualize the ant figuring out how to transverse a pebble which, in its frame of reference, is a veritable bolder. The ant has to take many inputs from its antennae (smell), eyes (light) and body (touch, vibration, feel and temperature), internalize that information and compare with what it has in memory (try going around, over or dig under) and output a decision. Moving up the complexity scale is the previous dog and rattle snake example.

Human decision making and behavior also falls into this category and is perhaps more complex. For example, a husband and wife are getting ready for a weekend, when the husband asks the wife, "Is it OK if I go out with the guys on Saturday."

Seeing his wife's obvious disappointment and conflict with her preplanned 'honey do' list for his weekend, she turns to the oldest trick in the book. "Fine (sighing), go out with your friends while I am here ... by myself."

This is a daunting computational task to say the least for any husband, particularly newbies. Churning in his mind he thinks, "Does she really mean stay or go? What would happen if I go? What will happen if I stay? How will she treat me if I go or stay?" And on and on. Furthermore, there may not be one right answer. Thus, these situations require extraordinarily complex processing. Perhaps, it is not until one has achieved the true path of enlightenment and wisdom that the answer to this eternal conundrum becomes apparent. I leave this answer to life's mysteries and for readers to discover.

Serious thought about computation and what it means in reality is a lesser known field of science to the masses. This is unfortunate because it has some profound discoveries for understanding our Universe. From the time Alan Turing proved the possibility of Universality, or the fundamental ability for a system to be able to emulate ANY OTHER SYSTEM; computational scientists have questioned what does this mean in the grand scheme of things (71). Can we emulate a human, the World, the Galaxy...the Universe? Wolfram states what Universality is in relation to real systems in his treatise, New Kind of Science (58):

> *"The basic point is, that if a system is universal, then it must effectively be capable of emulating any other system, and as a result it must be able to produce behavior that is as complex as the behavior of any other system. So knowing that a particular system is universal thus immediately implies that the system can produce behavior that is in a sense arbitrarily complex."*

The main point Wolfram makes is worth repeating. If a system is universal, then it can produce arbitrarily complex behavior. This point suggests that computers, designed from universality Turing Machine principles, should have the ability to emulate essentially anything. Wolfram later presents a Universal cellular automaton, which can perform **any** mathematical or logical computation (58).

Right about now you may be thinking, "Slow down! How does Universality affect the 'real' world or 'spiritual' world?" First off, there are no boundaries between the physical world and the hardware and software creating a 'computational' world. The hardware is based on physical principles and the behavior of the flowing electrons across it by instruction based logic better known as software. Wolfram's statement implies that if one looks at reality, through the eyes of a computational, interactive and informational perspective, any system that displays Class IV complex behavior invariably has the ability to emulate or model the **most** complex systems. Furthermore, Wolfram's Principle of Computational Equivalence suggests, *'...that in the end the vast majority of systems whose behavior is not obviously simple will turn out to be universal.'* Later in Chapter 12 he finalizes, *'...in fact almost any system whose behavior is not obviously simple performs computations that are in the end exactly equivalent in their sophistication.'*

This simply means that **any** universal, complex behaving systems are, computationally speaking, just as sophisticated as the **most** complex behaving systems. It then follows that a complex adaptive computational system, such as our nervous system, has the ability to model the behavior of **anything**! Anything? Yes, anything, including the entire Earth, The Milky Way Galaxy or even the most complex adaptive system known to humanity, the Universe! It is this fact, that suggests spiritually that we can become in touch with the divine flow, it is possible to have chaos limited predictability of the near future and we can fathom the Source, even if but for one brief moment.

This is where major resistance and arguments arise, such as, "You are trying to suggest that my little mind can model the entire Universe, and in essence know Source I can barely compute my checkbook let alone the whole Universe." This is an excellent point! If we can model anything, why do we not have godlike omni-prescience informing us of what is happening a million light years away? The answer lies with capacity and speed. We may be computationally equivalent to the entire Universe; however, we are far from physically or informationally equivalent. What do I mean by that? From a purely computational perspective, we are insignificant just like a universal cellular automata system on a computer, yet simultaneously, we are as complex and grand as the entire Universe. Physically, however, our personal system boundary (a.k.a. our body) compared with the rest of the Universe is vastly limited by our inputs (senses), outputs (energy, chemicals and sounds) and degree of networking and memory within our mind. We simply have less information and capacity with which to determine what is happening everywhere in the Universe. In addition, our computational speed is tremendously slow compared to the Universe as we shall see in the following exercises.

Thought Exercises:

1. If I have a computer that runs at 5 MHz (5,000,000 Hz) and another that runs at 1.5 GHz (1,500,000,000 Hz), which one would compute the answer to an equation that I posed to it faster? Which one would be able to control a system, such as a robot, more smoothly and quickly to inputs?

2. Let's say we build two robots with Universal computational processing units for their brain. Now let's say that Robot #1 has a single camera for vision, one microphone for auditory input and can move via four wheels. Robot #2 has two cameras for stereo vision, two microphones for stereo auditory input, artificial tactile sensors all over its exterior, an electrochemical nose and taste systems and temperature sensors. Robot #2 also has all of the degrees of freedom that the human body has for movement and locomotion. Which one could model the world around them more accurately?

3. Which Robot would model the world more like humans do? How does our human form affect our internal model of the world around us?

As far as we know, the Universe is computationally and informationally speaking massive if not infinite. We can model the Universe as a causal network starting from an assumed initial condition (i.e. the Big Bang or specific time point in a cyclical Universe). Let's assume that it 'sub-atomically conducts information at the speed of light, c, presumably at the fastest speed we know, light speed (~300,000,000 m/s or perhaps faster if entanglement theory holds). Furthermore, the fastest clock rates directly measured are up to 1×10^{19} Hz (~10,000,000,000,000,000,000 Hz or 10 Million THz). Indirectly measured these rates appear to be intermittently much higher during cosmic air shower events (72).

Another study of entanglement information transmission suggests the speed of quantum information transfer to be at a *minimum* of 15000 times the speed of light or 450,000,000,000 m/s. (73) The fastest computer on the planet or even the entire computational ability of the Earth would **not** be able to match that speed or throughput that the Universal photon or entanglement networks operate. *In order to predict what was happening everywhere in the Universe at all times and spaces, one would have to BE the Universe.* In addition, one still would model only the present, albeit with an omnipotent vantage point. Thus, it is not surprising that our brains, which informationally process at a relatively sluggish ionic conduction rates around 240 mph (101 m/s) with firing cycles around 200 Hz, are completely ill equipped for the task of modeling the Universe (74). We easily become overwhelmed when contemplating the Universe with all of its complexity.

We do however; have the Universal network structure within our atoms at the very core of our being. Therefore, from a logical and spiritual perspective, if it is within us, we should be able to interact with it. Perhaps this is what happens when we get glimpses of clarity, feel a wave of knowing or experience an epiphany of purpose when imagining our role in the cosmos. This also suggests in order for us to even attempt to tap into this flow, we need to quiet our normal brain noise at the ionic conduction level so we can be more present to the subatomic network. It is no irony then that the practice of meditation in all of its forms seeks to quiet the mind, so that the Universal network or Tao in eastern philosophy can be heard and listened to.

Most science and engineering create technology inspired by nature. The demonstration of entanglement is not just limited to a few special cases; it is constantly being reproduced in labs around the world using not only photons, but also now mechanical oscillators. According to Scientific American, as of June 3, 2010, the record for the longest distance between entangled photons is 144 km, between the Canary Islands of La Palma and Tenerife (75). In addition, the National Institute of Standards and Technology (NIST), has produced entangled mechanical oscillators using coupled atoms that could be incorporated into nano-technology and ultra fast and secure communications technology (76). These developments suggest that if we can repeatedly reproduce these quantum entanglements in the lab and in technology, nature probably has several conditions where quantum entanglement happens naturally.

While quantum entanglement seems to have a growing body of reproducible evidence to support the theory, a classical physicist argument against entanglement is that faster than light information transfer violates general relativity. The theory of general relativity limits the acceleration of a mass to exactly the speed of light in a vacuum, because it would require an infinite amount of energy to accelerate any mass to the speed of light. This holds true if information is transferred using a 'mass particle'. A counter argument holds that information transfer does not necessarily require a 'mass particle' and thus a single bit of information can transfer via massless interactions with minimal energy requirements, perhaps even none. Computational quantum physicists are beginning to think that the computational properties of the Universe may be better described by laws that govern information rather than laws that govern matter, because they have repeated several experiments teleporting photons, atoms, ions and now energy (77). These ideas are the basis for what I call quantum information entanglement transfer or QUIET. QUIET presents an idea that information is a coupling dimension that permeates traditional space-time. Thus, quantum informational causality using qubits and physical information causality using bits may co-exist. In fact, many trails of research into quantum computing and information processing, too numerous to dive into here, indeed suggest transfer of information in two very different ways at two different speeds (75) (51) (77) (49) (44) (73) (50) (78).

It is no wonder that since the dawn of humankind people have been trying to find a way to connect to and become one with this stream of informational flow, or universal consciousness. People want to feel connected to the grand complex adaptive system, most call by a name (God, Brahma, Allah, Yahweh, Buddha, Zen, Tao or other unifying idea or entity) and science calls the Universe. Any name, with which we label such an infinite system, by its very nature, is inadequate. Thus most of us are tied to a limited, anthropomorphic metaphor of the infinite at best. It is the most expansive, complex and intense informational flow knowable, the weave which creates and sustains our very fabric of being, the Source. Science has come full circle, forcing us to face the new reality and redefine our existence.

CHAPTER 7
THE EMERGENT SPIRIT

-Man's mind, once stretched by a new idea,
never regains its original dimensions-

Oliver Wendell Homes Author & physician (1809 - 1894)

THE REDEFINED LIFE OF NATURE

From this point in the text forward, I will capitalize grouping pronouns throughout the book, such as 'We', 'Us' and 'Our'. Capitalization of these specific pronouns is not a random grammatical accident just to get a rise out of English teachers everywhere, my wife included, but is intended to foster a new way of thinking about existence based upon insights 11-15, listed again below:

11. We are never separate from the flow of consciousness, or It us.
12. Nothing separates Us from one another or the Cosmos, We only believe it is so.
13. The more you align yourself and others with divine flow the greater the influence either by intention, attention or entanglement.
14. The complex dance of Life and Universe, as an integrated whole, is eternally played out between order and disorder revealing a divine unfolding.

15. All naturally occurring CAS, and by implication all Life, simultaneously emerge from smaller agents of scale and contribute to a larger emergent being as agents.

The prime reason is to emphasize the fact that We are inseparable parts of a whole forming the emergent entity Humanity. Thus a simple language modification, within this text, is not only a way to recognize this convention, but actualizes the unity principle. Proven by the very foundations of logic and scientific knowledge We conclude the following insight.

Insight #16: We are of One and the same Source.

This insight is not a new idea; it has always resonated with Humanity since the dawn of civilization. Now We have a body of positive proof to reinvigorate and renew the concept. Consider the history behind this monumental piece of wisdom. It took the human race, using integrative and reductionist tools of the scientific method, eons to rediscover this outcome. We are One and the same in Our very fabric of existence. Paradoxilly, We are also complex and adaptive enough, at an individual level, to self organize into organic distinguishable forms We recognize as Our bodies. What an amazing duality of existence! *Human beings are an orchestrated paradox of order and disorder, matter and energy, inseparable yet distinguishable.*

Such a revelation also suggests that We are One and the same with all Life in Our city, state and country. Even what We classify as nonlife is included in the mix, because all matter and energy dances to similar rhythms at quantum and atomic scales. Indeed the entire planet Earth, named Gaia, from the ancient Greek Goddess of the same name, by John Lovelock, is an extension of Us. Gaia is Our emergent living body that Humanity is an integral part. We are the agents (cells). We have worker 'cells', thinker 'cells', fighter 'cells', nutrient transfer 'cells', and on and on (61) (63).

The Milky Way Galaxy and the entire Universe are supersets that include the Earth and Us. Thus Our fundamental connection between all things (matter, energy and information) is not just a 'nice idea' it's a verifiable requirement. Therefore, We refer to a collective or the singular by name. Humanity has done this since the dawn of language.

With this new focus on the networked interactions rather than separate entities, We gain a perspective that 'We' and 'Us' are just as valid formal names of a collection of interacting minds as is Juan or Xiao-Lee or James. For example, the interaction of you reading this book, independent of my writing of it, has set up a communication interaction between Us, the named pronoun I'm using to describe this ongoing process.

You may be thinking right now, "Wow, what is this guy thinking? Does this make any sense in 'reality'?" Excellent question!

Thought Exercise:

Consider this. You have a name for yourself, such as, Bob, for argument's sake. Feel free to insert your name in place of 'Bob' for this exercise. What does 'Bob' really describe? Is it your body, the body of Bob? Is it perhaps your stomach, hungry Bob? Well now that seems absurd; the stomach is part of the body of Bob of course. (Side note: neurophysiologists and noetic scientists have evidence that the stomach has somewhat a mind of its own called the enteric nervous system, which is apparently, influenced by outside remote psi stimuli such as strong emotions) (79). "Aha," you say, "the brain. Bob is the brains of the operation." So, I ask you, "What is the brain?"

Either you have some previous knowledge of the brain or perhaps you quickly Google the answer (Notice Google is also capitalized like all company names which is a collection of people and materials, which is interesting since Google is now simultaneously a noun and a verb). Something like the following definition comes up in your search. "The brain is a collection of neurons and glial support cells comprising both the white and grey matter." Not much help.

Perhaps Bob is the area of the brain and body responsible for collectively controlling bodily functions. Is that not a collection of interacting cells? Are you the Bob collective? What about the mind, is the mind named Bob? The best neuroscience has come up with is that the mind is a series of continuous interactions in chaotic cycles associated with collective thoughts. It is still unclear what generates these cycles. In fact, Stuart Hameroff, Roger Penrose and many others that study and model the brain have found that the microtubules in the glial cells and neurons have far more computing power per neuron than We ever knew (80).

Furthermore, diving into this area of research, you discover the Hameroff-Penrose model which postulates microtubule 'mers' (repeating molecular unit in the microtubule) participate in quantum level events and may actually be the seed of consciousness in the human brain. They hypothesize that quantum collapse allows Us to perceive the apparent forward arrow of time. In addition, according to Mavromatos et. al., these nanostructures may act as an ideal quantum setting at physiologic temperatures for entanglement to occur on time scales of perception (81). More research into these topics is ongoing with ideas of biophotonic waveguides and quantum teleportation models, so We shall see what the future holds. These theories and studies are creating a new gateway into the mind, suggesting that the mind may coexist with the brain, but not require it. Furthermore, if the mind does not require the brain to operate then it opens the possibility that it exists beyond the dying brain. What then? Have We found the soul of Bob? Is Bob the stuff of quantum interaction? Where did the separation of Bob from the rest of the Universe go? We again come full circle. Alas, We discover again that there indeed is NO SEPARATION!

Finally the ultimate question, if all my systems, agents and matter, are just made up of smaller interacting agents transferring information at the quantum level, what am I? Without such interactions, I as a whole, would collapse and cease to exist. Am I the emergent entity of my components or am I the collective of the interactions themselves?

Answering this question may seem an obvious at first but the more you look at it, it is the same basic question that physicist for centuries have been dueling with. *Is the fundamental makeup of the Universe 'stuff' called matter (objects) or is it the interactions between the 'stuff' (matter, energy, or something else)*? I propose and believe the answer lies within the interactions themselves. We already know that life cannot exist without change (a.k.a. interactions) and the state to state observations are as short as Planck's time scale. If We could theoretically stop all interactions between all agents at all levels of scale, simultaneously, and measure the state of every particle, agent, life form and entity, *actual existence would cease to... well exist*! We have stopped all informational transfer. Nothing or 'no-thing' can happen. Therefore, We conclude that in order for continued existence, information must flow and interactions at all scales *are* the mechanisms of action. Without interactions, I cannot strike this keyboard. You cannot read. I cannot think. You cannot see. We cannot BE physically, mentally or spiritually.

Insight #17: We are a localized flow of information within the universal flow of information.

The entirety of Our nature, Our very substance, energy, soul or spirit, if you like, is based upon the principle of interactions. Interactions qualify as such if there is information transferred between agents. Otherwise, no interaction has occurred. Through this inductive reasoning, ***I propose that the only difference between Our body, mind and spirit is the scale and nature of interactions between agents.***

The human ***body*** is essentially made up of eukaryotic cells interacting cooperatively in a way that creates the emergent organism. Neuroscience research has repeatedly proven that interactions between neuronal and glial cells, via ions and molecules, continually occur within the collective nervous system. Think about a specific memory or visualize performing a task in the future. This very moment your brain fires a multitude of synchronized cycles in groups of neurons. These synchronistic patterns permeate the network of your brain representing a multitude of simultaneous CAS actions. At this scale, the central nervous system (CNS) activity gives rise to the ***mind*** as the emergent entity. Perform a simple search through neuroscience articles related to mind, memory and thinking. You will find literally thousands of excellent peer reviewed works on these topics. (If you are interested in the latest research, go to www.pubmed.org or Journal of Neuroscience www. jneurosci.org/, both of which are great resources.)

Following a similar train of thought, if the spirit or soul is another emergent system, what kinds of agents are at work with it? The answer to this question may in fact be what quantum level physics is uncovering. I submit a plausible hypothesis:

*The **spirit, soul** or **essence** may in fact be the emergent entity arising from Planck's scale level interactions, which create local (and perhaps entangled global) informational and memory loops.*

The emergent ***spirit*** may be a massless informational construct not necessarily bound by space-time limitations. The 'soul' is then formed from a network of subatomic particle information exchanges at the quantum or Planck's scale. It is no wonder when we learn or experience something new (i.e. gain information), we feel like we grow. At our most fundamental level, we are growing! We are growing in spirit. This may explain humanity's craving for knowledge; it is as necessary as breathing.

The result is astonishing. As We discussed seemingly unrelated topics as relativistic and quantum physics, entangled minds, information transfer and computational equivalence of complex systems, a possible logical and yet spiritually profound explanation emerged. The theory integrates these elusive phenomena, at their most basic levels, under one banner. The counter argument is that they are not related; and thus, We continue pursuing independent phenomena paths. At the very least this strategy has left many people confounded, uninspired and lacking purpose. At the very worst, humanity stands in conflict with Our very nature.

In order for this theory to have merit, We need to obtain a deeper understanding this phenomenon. Interdisciplinary scientists need to research information reactions. One interesting question in this direction being studied is, 'Do informational interactions require energy like their mass interaction counterparts?' Ostrowski suggests that a minimum amount of energy is used to copy one bit of "classical" information in the presence of noise, thus generating the apparent flow of time from past to future (82). However, Milan Ćirković and Miroljub Dugić investigated the distinction between "classical" and "quantum" information and found that "zero average energy quantum information processing is possible." (83) Furthermore, Joan Vaccaro from the University of Brisbane in Australia and Stephen Barnett from the University of Strathclyde in the UK found it possible to erase information without energy cost (84). If quantum information interactions indeed require no net energy, thereby hinting at potentially no mass requirement, then these findings bolster the theory presented in this chapter.

How can this be? From the second law of thermodynamics, the conventional assumption is all things require energy and the flow is always in the direction of greater entropy or disorder. The second law holds thus far, for terrestrial electrical, chemical and mechanical interactions. Otrowski suggests that the second law of thermodynamics, which is usually associated with the forward progression of time or the "arrow of time", is more of a function of a minimal amount of energy for observing this quantum soup of activity (85). The act of observation requires a "classical" copy of the "quantum" information thus giving rise to the observation of past. Since the future is in the constant state of creation, any little tweak to a complex adaptive system will change the outcome. This prevents exact fortune telling via a "memory" of the future with "classical" information giving Us a sense of time progression usually associated with the second law. It is unknown if this same limitation exists for purely "quantum" information without observation.

As an engineer, this law was pounded into Us as undergraduate students. In contrast and probably one of the most fascinating aspects of complexity science is the phenomenon of emergence or 'order from disorder'. Emergent forms, as we looked at in Chapter 6, are patterns and complex systems seem to counteract the very entropy suggested in the second law. Such order is evident in all life forms, planets, stars, galaxies and pure mathematical cellular automata (63) (57) (61) (58).

Up till now, I distilled mountains of scientific, mathematical and philosophical information down to a digestible amount. I fear some of the amazing stories of discovery and shear awe may be lost due to this process. I tried to summarize pivotal findings that I find fascinating and inspiring. However, it may not be the trigger that sets your mind a blaze with new ideas and awareness. Please, I encourage you to follow your path down some of these rabbit holes. Look up some of the provided works cited. Start your own investigation. Find your own evidence for something greater, so that you can better appreciate first-hand or 'noetic' information.

Now that you have a place to start, what do you do with this new found path? How do We wake up every day and realign ourselves with this expanded reality?

EMBRACE EXPANSION

-If I could define enlightenment briefly, I would
say it is the quiet acceptance of what is.

−Dr. Wayne Dyer

The largest obstacle for most people today is complacency. People resist refining or redefining their belief systems. I believe the reasons for this conflict, which lies within most of Us, stems from the fear discussed in Chapters 2 and 3 earlier. That is why, before discussing fascinating and compelling discoveries happening around the world, I addressed this issue upfront in an attempt to open your mind.

If you want to know how to find the keys accessing enlightenment, it has never been further than your own mind. Simply, open the door of your mind. Integrate the new with the old. If there is conflict between ideas try to resolve it. If you need to throw out old ideas because they no longer make sense, do so. I don't suggest that you believe everything that comes your way without question, but I do suggest that everyone become a *spiritual scientist* and use the newly emergent mind that you now have. Systematically, logically and experientially test all information that comes your way. The true Divine Source has no qualms with questions being asked for the sake of enlightened discovery. A Divine omnipotent Source should, by definition, stand up to any amount of scrutiny mustered up by little ol' humanity. There are no laws written anywhere saying otherwise.

Something written 1700+ years ago does not have any more insight or validity into the very nature of what you are than anything written today. Ancient people didn't know more about the Universe around you than people now. In fact, the opposite is true! We have far more information easily available to Us now on the nature of the Universe and ourselves than ever before! If We plan on continuing to Spiritually Evolve as a species and a planet as a whole, We need to keep integrating the new with the old. Not create an even larger chasm between the two. I call this the **Integration Process**.

> *Insight #18: Embracing universal knowledge is like panning for gold. Filter through mud all day and perhaps you find a nugget of wisdom. Ironically, even if you do not find the golden truth you seek, you still gain wisdom through knowing where not to look and joy through adventure.*

The Integration Process- Guiding steps for encountering new spiritual information:

1. Upon acquiring credible information or wisdom, incorporate it into your emerging model.

2. If information does not fit due to some discrepancy, be it large or small; look to find the source of the discrepancy.
3. If the discrepancy cannot be resolved directly, the information you are incorporating is either flawed, your model is flawed or the method of integration is incorrect.
4. Be open to any of these possibilities and don't reject a compelling golden nugget just because it may require a serious revamp your view of the Universe.
5. When the discrepancies are too large to resolve by the steps above and you are facing serious personal resistance, cycle back to the edge of the chasm in Chapter 2.
6. Remove any new anchors that are the source of resistance
7. Once again, take the leap.

With practice, you will find that Integration Process gets easier and easier. Eventually, the concept of integrating new information in your life will be as floating on a river. The secret is to let go of expectations.

LETTING GO OF PRECONCEIVED PLANS

As with any worthwhile journey, the best experiences are the adventures that We have when Our plans go awry. I made big plans for proposing to my wife over a decade ago. I preplanned everything! We were to arrive at a magical timeshare in Steamboat Springs, Colorado in the warm spring air. I was going to whisk her up to the tallest mountain peak, riding a tram to get there. When I had her all to myself, I was going to poetically perform my rehearsed lines upon one knee with the ring miraculously emerging from nowhere. She would be amazed and surprised by my planning prowess and could not say no.

Now it would not be a story if that is the way it went. Unbeknown to me in the course of my planning, it was the month of May, which to those unsuspecting Colorado vacation planners means

"Mud season". The weatherman had predicted warm spring like conditions. However, as we passed through Durango on our way to Steamboat Springs, it began to snow. Being from the Phoenix area, we had packed for spring, not winter. Furthermore, when we arrived at are destination, everything, I MEAN EVERYTHING, was closed, including the resort and Sky tram where I was going to take her up to the peak. Since climbing four thousand feet was not exactly her idea of romance, I secretively, but desperately looked into horseback riding up a portion of the way, but that too was closed. After a day of not plans going awry, we stopped by a Starbucks to get a beverage. Guess what, also closed; I didn't see that one coming.

I started to panic a bit as my entire plan was crumbling around me and my wife to be started questioning, "Who is this strange man next to me, and what did he do with my boyfriend?" Finally, we get back to the timeshare; go out to the deck overlooking the mountain range and I decide to muster the courage to recite my lines. But no! I cannot remember a single syllable. I have given talks to hundreds of people, performed on the stage in high school and I cannot get it together to recite a few lines to the one woman it mattered to most. I had to run back to my backpack to retrieve the lines and then convince my wife that she needed to look at the mountains. "Crazy man," she's thinking to herself.

Finally, I read off my lines from a scribbled piece of paper and give her the ring, wrapped in a receipt I had been holding in my pocket for two days. Once the significance of the moment of what I was trying to do and after almost dropping the ring off the balcony three stories up, she burst into tears of joy. I asked her if she was OK and she replied that it all makes sense now and was relieved that I, in fact, was not crazy as she was beginning to believe.

We kissed, got married several months later and have an even better story to tell than if everything when according to my "master plan".

Let go of expectations! This is a fundamental precept in yogic practice. If you explore the inner self and outer cosmos with expectation of a specific outcome, you'll face only met or unmet expectations. Either way, you are confining possibilities to a convenient and compartmentalized human viewpoint. Keep room open for the completely unplanned.

The most amazing way to journey through modern spiritual emergence is to not have ANY expectations! Observe with the sense and wonder of a child, since We truly are children of the Universe. Show gratitude for every experience that furthers your understanding of the Divine Source. My father said to us when things did not go according to plan, "There are no good or bad events in life, only experiences. I hope to give you many."

There is no separate external (out there) or internal (in here). What you find 'out there' can be found within and vice versa. The Integral Process is the state of returning to your childlike mind, your innocence. Continually revel in amazement. The main difference between childhood and now is you have a wakened mind with more tools to get to know your Universe, the Divine Source.

DISCOVER PERSONAL MORAL RESPONSIBILITY

-Choice emerges with consciousness-

Harold J. Morowitz (Former Editor in Chief of the Journal Complexity and Co-chair of the Science board of the Santa Fe Institute)

With great insight comes great responsibility. Our free will comes with a price. Just as an adult is freer than a child to do as they wish, she is also more responsible for her life and the lives of those she interacts with. This may be where science parts with some Eastern traditions of Zen Buddhism and other passive philosophies. We not only have ethical responsibilities and rules that govern daily interactions with one another, but We also need to follow Our collective moral compass. Before We can collectively move forward with moral purpose, We need to revisit the past.

The Universe contained the seed of an emerging consciousness from the moment collective forms emerged from the formless. From the moment a multi-cellular organism occurs, the seed of emergence begins. According to modern evolutionary science, the emergence of will or 'volition' corresponds with the emergence of the *mind* (86). It took eons for reptiles to evolve, then mammals, and more recently the subset of primates which adapted and evolved into the modern human form (87). All of these forms have varied levels of *mind* complexity.

The act of volition; however, requires a *mind* to learn, remember and change behavioral response to an event as a result (88). All prior emergent life forms have or had levels of volition. On Earth, it was not until the arrival of early life that species began to model the environment around them. This ability required simple neural networked processing systems and biological sensors. To some extent all species attempt to predict outcomes based on several possible actions, hence the emergence of cause and effect reasoning in people.

Meanwhile for millions of years, before and during the time it took for humans to arrive, the Earth body and mind was simultaneously emerging. Theories of life's interdependence with and hence emergence of Earth have been formally developed by James Lovelock and others over the last few decades. Most famous names used for the theory are 'Gaia Theory' or 'Gaia Hypothesis' (70).

Science has been acutely aware of the thermodynamic and biochemical Gaia *Body* interdependence with all life on the planet. What if, in addition, We view Our individual consciousness as integral with all other consciousnesses on the planet (human or otherwise)? We can then envision and create an emergent global consciousness or the '*mind*' of Gaia.

Is this preposterous to propose? Consider that We know everything is informationally and causally linked to everything else in the greater Universe, so why wouldn't humanity be connected to the planet at large? It is highly plausible Our network of interlinked consciousnesses, particularly with human advancement of the internet and telecommunications, is collectively the '***mind***' of Our very planet, Earth.

This would be a stunning revelation. Particularly since humanity may be the only species with enough knowledge and capability to save this planet. Awareness of this concept, drives home Our collective responsibility and stewardship to Earth. If We are at the core of the Earth mind, We are the feedback and control system required to help the Earth continue far into the future. We only require the will to act.

If We extend this theory to everything, We are an integral part (albeit smaller portion) of the '***mind***' of the entire Universe, the grandest of all universal complex adaptive systems known. At this scale Our role is somewhat of a mystery. Like all good mysteries, perhaps the path to discovering the mystery is the role We play.

Insight #19: Literally, whether We believe in it or not, We are an inseparable part of the Mind of God, the Source.

The human mind is known to be an individual consciousness created from trillions upon trillions of interacting quantum events, within and beyond the networked constructs of Our brain. Also, there is no quantum interaction boundary between humans and every other being, plant, rock, matter and photon in the Universe. Therefore, We conclude that the *'Earth Mind'* is the emergent superset of the planet and the *'Universal Mind'* is the ultimate emergent superset!

If Insight 19 sounds similar to Insight 16; it is. They are similar in presenting people as a subset of the whole Universe. The difference is Insight 16 discusses physical interactions mostly between masses and particles; Insight 19 describes the seamless integration of information flow particularly at the quantum level. The distinction is subtle but profound. It suggests that there are simultaneously a physical (Universal Body) and mental (Universal Mind) at work within the same space. This duality is familiar to Us, since people experience a similar phenomenon within Our own bodies.

Let's step back a moment. Where does morality fit into this equation? What are the implications of you and I being interconnected with everything else? The very fact that We are all weaved from the same cloth helps clarify that We are of one divine being we call Universe or Source. When We harm another We harm ourselves in some foreseeable or unforeseeable way. Thus Insight 19 gives Us pause. We must evaluate Our actions between each other and this world more critically. If someone you see decides to take an aggressive or violent action against another being, human or otherwise, consider the direct and indirect consequences. Chances are, that aggression will propagate and come back to haunt the perpetrator but the rest of society as well. Most philosophies and religions recognize this effect, such as Karma in Buddhism or Hindu practices.

Many Native American Indians and other tribal cultures also understood this basic notion when it came to necessary violence. When hunting animals, for example, the hunter gave thanks and gratitude for the sacrifice of life so that his tribe could live. In the modern western world and the industrialization of food sources, only phantoms of these traditions remain, such as 'Saying Grace' and Thanksgiving. According the American Thanks-Giving Foundation, pre-Columbus American Indians are attributed with the quote *"The plant has its nourishment from the earth and its limbs go up this way, in praise of its Maker ... like the limbs of a tree."* (89) In fact rituals of 'Gratitude' go back to prehistoric man and an official 'Thanks-Giving' day is practiced in over eight nations.

Since all plants, animals and people are integral to the Mind and Body of the Source, We need to appreciate, respect and protect one another. We sacrifice what is necessary for survival and no more. More results in gluttony, which in turn harms all life. How do We see this in real life? Overfishing of our oceans is a tragic example of how greed is coming back to haunt humanity. We have lost an estimated 90% of Our fish population in the ocean within the past 50 years. Certain species of sharks have been hit particularly hard with a decrease of 97% (90). Overfishing by industrialized countries is also leading to a shortage of food for the developing world leading to starvation in fishing cultures that have long relied on sustainable fishing for their survival (91). In short, if We revere ALL and respect ALL as part of the Source, then everyday is a gift.

So am I not to eat plants or animals because they are part of the Source? Not at all, every species and entity will strive to survive. Here is what I am saying. *Do not take food, clothing, shelter or companionship for granted OR in excess of what is required.* Why? Because there is a cost to lives elsewhere for everything you consume. You may not see it or be aware of it immediately, but is a natural consequence. Likewise when others consume they are directly or indirectly affecting you. Therefore, consume wisely because you are only borrowing these goods. When your body dies, it too will be recycled back into the loop. As We learned from the tombs of the richest Pharaohs of ancient Egypt, all Our wealth, wine, cloths, servants and luxuries don't go with Us. An enlightened being, knows to not waist precious time purely on acquiring luxurious illusions. She instead focuses on positive interactions with all they come in contact with, and abundance follows.

Insight # 20: An enlightened life exists within the interactions not the states in which they produce.

CHAPTER 8
ENLIGHTENMENT-A
PATH NOT A PLACE

Divine Moment

> *-There is infinity in a wave...a flame...or air through trees. Why else are We so easily transfixed on the serene without awareness of time or space? As We reach for comprehension of the majesty before Us, We cannot fathom the sheer magnitude of Our minuteness to the divine. Yet inexplicably, We are drawn to and lifted by the realization that We too are of this nature...this essence We call existence. In that moment, We taste forever...immortal.-*

As we journeyed through Chapters 1 through 7, We have treaded through seeming treacherous waters of the unknown. We felt the drowning fear threatening to drag us down and then reemerged with new insight. Our minds emerged with a compelling sense that there is much more to this journey.

I am sure you started this book with various expectations of the outcome. Perhaps you sought answers to deep questions or wished to reaffirm knowledge that you may have felt, but did not have the resources or time to look into. Others dove into this work with the full intention of discrediting ideas, yet if you are still reading this, I submit that you have indeed changed. Perhaps the best question for you now is how have you changed? Are you better for it? What questions have you answered? What new questions now saturate your thoughts?

These are all profound experiences which require an answer. The answer is you have discovered a **Path of Enlightenment**. Notice

I did not say 'the' Path of Enlightenment, since that would suggest that there is only one Path. I have no evidence to suggest a singular Path. Another name that is used is "*The Way.*" These terms '*Path*' and '*Way*' come from Eastern philosophical practice and seem to best encapsulate the *process* of what is transpiring while minimizing any overt religious connotations. Through this *process*, have you gotten somewhere? Perhaps. More commonly people realize they have arrived at one peak along a mountain range. There are many, perhaps infinite, peaks and higher peaks to explore.

The important concept to understand here is that enlightenment is not a *state of being*; it is an *awakening process, path or way* in which you lead your life. I emphasize that last part, "**...you lead your life.**" The enlightened self, can no longer operate off of a purely programmed past, based upon what others have told them. From now on, you proceed in a "noetic" or experiential way. Reactions to present circumstances, whether for good or ill, don't need to be defined by the past.

THE WAY OF NOW.

> -*Nothing ever happened in the past; it happened in the Now.*
> *Nothing will ever happen in the future; it will happen in the Now.*
>
> - *Eckhart Tolle*

Most unawakened people journey through life reacting to the world around them. They substantially set blame for their circumstances on other people, situations or external factors. This is not to say that external events don't have any effect on their lives. They do. Instead, an enlightened soul, following 'The Way', *does not let the external events <u>control</u> his actions*. He deals with matters of the present as they come and projects immediate future outcomes, usually for the benefit of others as well as themselves. There are many eastern cultures that have learned and taught this process over eons.

Ironically, the modern westernized world seems to have substantially, although not entirely, lost this ability. Too many people blame their current behavior and circumstance on their abusive childhood, missing parents, gangs, war, violence, video games. To live this reactionary way of life is to be a prisoner to your ego and your very memories. Tread carefully. It's easy to fall into the memory trap.

How do we avoid the memory trap? First learn to recognize it. The trap subtly begins within by projecting past thoughts directly onto the present situation. Learned fears and emotions cloud the realm of possible actions. Then the ego leads to you reacting rashly in a preprogrammed manner.

The practice of Zen essentially helps break this past-present trapping of the mind. Eckhart Tolle's book, *The Power of Now*, is a concise modernization of many Zen techniques which teach Us how to remove ourselves from this incessant loop. According to Tolle, the essence of living is within the gap, not governed by the past or your ego (92). This gap or space allows you to create free will for yourself. This idea resonates with Our previous thought that the essence of spirit exists in the information flow between states, not in the states themselves. Interestingly, some neurologists trained in western medicine argue that you <u>don't</u> have free will because a neuron is required to fire to create free will. Thus, We are all slaves to Our genetically programmed responses. This argument is limited and fails from several of the following facts.

1. Modern neuroscience has mountains of evidence that the brain and subsequently "living mind" is plastic and reprogrammable with practice or attention (93). (If you are interested, a thorough search on any valid Neuroscience journal will reveal a plethora of evidence.)
2. Consciousness has been related to quantum events within and outside the scope of the biological structures (e.g. microtubules) (80).
3. Meditative and martial art practices not only enhance brain function, but help individuals modify their own behaviors (94).

Being in 'the gap' simply means, observe your mind, body and surroundings. Practice the art of 'witnessing' your very thoughts. Subtly quiet the incessant voice in your head that analyzes every moment. By mastering this skill, you empower yourself to literally jump out of the situation you are experiencing into an objective, peaceful 'gap'. From this gap, exercise 'free-will' by *choosing* the response instead of reacting with an ego driven emotional response.

This practice is ancient and common among Eastern Buddhist philosophies. When taking Tai Chi back in college, my teacher taught Us many valuable Chinese martial arts philosophies. One particular lesson is encapsulated in the following story:

> The Master says to his student, 'A Dragon can always defeat a Tiger even if the Tiger knows all the Dragons forms.'
>
> The student looks at his master quizzically and asks, 'Why is this so, The Tiger knows all of the Dragon's forms'
>
> The Master replies, 'The Dragon understands when not to use them.'

In other words, the true master must not only master her body, but ultimately her mind. This is especially true for those wishing to stay on the path of enlightenment. The only way to follow the path is to master yourself and exercise your free will. As author and psychologist Dr. Wayne Dyer defines it, "Get into the gap". The next question becomes, "What do I do while on the path?"

COMPASSIONATE JOURNEY

> -Love and compassion are necessities, not luxuries. Without them humanity cannot survive. -Tenzin Gyatso, 14th Dalai Lama

Compassion is the key to opening the doorway to understanding. Understanding is the opportunity to create an experience of love and kindness. The experience of love and kindness passes the key on to the next person.

Imagine a world in which everyone practiced the above paragraph. If even one of Us conducts Our day in such a manner, and that person connects with 10 people that day, what an amazing difference that would make. If they, in turn, connect with 10 more, and so on, We would collectively create a positive cascade across the entire world. Imagine the changes that would happen. A day without War? Perhaps a pause in world hunger? Who knows? The possibilities are truly inspiring.

Many Tibetan monks live by this philosophy. Which begs the

question? If this global cascade effect is possible, why have humans not been able to translate such phenomenon into a global conscious experience? Perhaps We have to some extent and we just don't realize it. Another likely reason is that We too often interfere with negativity. This process is similar to stress and negative thinking in your own mind.

Psychologists have known for quite some time that negative thoughts block the positive endorphin experience that creates well being in your body. Similarly, the individual and collective need to cling to the past creates blockages to positive flow. Hate, vendettas and tragedies' of war, prevent the flow of compassion across all agents of the human collective consciousness. Ironically, people often decide to perpetuate these negative feelings by continually returning their attention back to tragedy. We memorialize it, perpetually blame others and cling to traditions that limit true societal healing.

Classic examples of this phenomenon are several ongoing battles over who is the rightful owner of some 'Holy Land' first. The argument is perpetually absurd and moot since the land belongs to no man. If anything the 'land' may claim ownership of Us. Our very molecules sprang from the land. The land existed long before any human 'claimed' it, and it will continue to exist long after Our species. Humanity either adapts and evolves or gets wiped from existence by Our unbending ineptitude. In reality, most of these arguments are not about what relic belongs to whom, but about who gets power and control. In this respect, it is very similar to patent law suits over intellectual property. Who gets to make money and control the idea? These conflicts completely miss the point of compassion and understanding. Furthermore such clashes proliferate continued hate, corruption and violence. In a nutshell, these tit-for-tat fights epitomize pure reason without true spirituality.

Although religion has often tried to hold spirituality hostage within the institution that dispenses it, people are trending away from such behavior in some faiths. At the time I am writing this book, Pope Benedict XVI in a speech on September 17th in Westminster Hall stated:

> *"The central question at issue, then, is this: where is the ethical foundation for political choices to be found? The Catholic*

> tradition maintains that the objective norms governing right
> action are accessible to reason, prescinding from the content of
> revelation. According to this understanding, the role of religion
> in political debate is not so much to supply these norms, as if
> they could not be known by non-believers – still less to propose
> concrete political solutions, which would lie altogether outside
> the competence of religion – but rather to help purify and shed
> light upon the application of reason to the discovery of objective
> moral principles. This "corrective" role of religion vis-à-vis reason
> is not always welcomed, though, partly because distorted forms
> of religion, such as sectarianism and fundamentalism, can be seen
> to create serious social problems themselves. And in their turn,
> these distortions of religion arise when insufficient attention
> is given to the purifying and structuring role of reason within
> religion. It is a two-way process. Without the corrective supplied
> by religion, though, reason too can fall prey to distortions, as
> when it is manipulated by ideology, or applied in a partial way
> that fails to take full account of the dignity of the human person.
> Such misuse of reason, after all, was what gave rise to the slave
> trade in the first place and to many other social evils, not least
> the totalitarian ideologies of the twentieth century. This is
> why I would suggest that the world of reason and the world of
> faith – the world of secular rationality and the world of religious
> belief – need one another and should not be afraid to enter into a
> profound and ongoing dialogue, for the good of our civilization."

Notice underlying themes in this portion of the Pope's speech.
First, Benedict XVI reveals concern for the dwindling power of
the Catholic Church's power by wishing to have ongoing dialog
with political institutions of the world. At face value, this merely
was an attempt to reinvigorate the Catholic's institutional role in
Britain's parliamentary process, but look more closely. The Pope
goes on to discuss the subtle understanding that religions can be
"distorted" by sectarianism and fundamentalism. More critically
he acknowledges the "misuse" of religion *or* reason can create
atrocities; such as the slave trade, for purely economic reasons.
Likewise, We have already discussed in previous chapters some of
the atrocities of religion without reason. I do offer my respect for this
revelation by the Pope. However, many other philosophies including
what is promoted here believe in true individual and collective
spirituality, governed by compassion. Compassion, practiced at
local and global scales, is a tool and perhaps prescription for many
of the global ills, such as economic greed, complacency and acts of

hatred. As German Philosopher, Arthur Schopenhauer once wrote, *"Compassion is the basis of all morality."* (95)

Insight #21: Compassion guides the enlightened mind along the path. Without it, the way is lost.

Therefore, I propose the governing principles for action is not governed by reason and religion alone, but in fact all action needs to be governed by *compassion*. Let's now consider very real present day examples of pure reason or pure religious actions and consequences without the guidance of compassion as previously mentioned by Pope Benedict XVI. We have to look no further than recent events.

Catastrophic capitalism, without checks and balances, is a perfect example of what happens when reason alone is used without spiritual or moral guidance. Unscrupulous investment banks and hedge funds, with help from 'reputable' rating agencies, created one of the most greed driven cash heists in history from the middle class and poor. Reason and evidence alone suggested financial institutions would earn a huge profit from bundling questionable home loans with good loans into bonds. These bonds were then separated and rebundled into new products called credit default swaps (CDS) hiding the obvious risk. At this point the rating agencies, such as Moody's, were paid by the very agencies that required rating of these CDSs which miraculously came up with the lowest risk rating of AAA. Had anyone actually looked underneath the hood of these CDSs, they would realize the high potential risk of them failing and would stand to make billions betting against them. In fact, this is what several hedge funds and investment banks, such as Goldman Sachs, actually did. A great expose on both the finance industry culture and rampant recklessness called "The Big Short" was written by former Wall Streeter Michael Lewis (35).

Had the finance industry tempered its greed with a sense of compassion and consequence of multibillion dollar decisions being orchestrated by so few individuals, it would have paused and reconsidered. Perhaps the financial decision makers would have thought about the down side of such actions. Ironically, the financial institutions had so obfuscated the real worth of their own products that ultimately their own analysts trick themselves into thinking that there was no downside. Does the saying "Seemed like a good idea at the time," sound prophetic?

The finance industries' cascading misdealings lead the world to the largest recession since the Great Depression of the 1930s. Were Our investment banks, lenders and loan originators compassionately thinking about the millions of people who were being duped into loans they could not possibly repay? Just because a corporation or hedge fund can make billions off the backs of the poor and middle class's lack of financial knowledge, does that justify creating an environment that made ~20-30 million families in America alone lose their homes and jobs?

A far more extreme example is the 1994 Rwandan uprising. The Hutus massacred around 800,000 Tutsis within 100 days in response to the Hutu President Juvenal Habyariman being shot. How compassionate were the extremist Hutus when killing innocent Tutsis civilians they perceived as a threat? Did the death of one man reasonably justify genocide? (25)

Instead of looking at the past, let's turn Our attention to future social instability. What will happen if We continue using spirituality or reason without compassion?

Research Exercise:

1. Perform an internet search on 'Spiritual warfare' and see what comes up.
2. Browse through some of the articles and try to access what message is being delivered.
3. See if the proprietors of such sights are working in Our best spiritual interest, or their religious agenda.

Objective observation of these web sites reveals extreme Christian and Muslim trends using elements of fear control, discussed in Chapter 2, suggesting that hell and damnation of your soul is at stake. But I have only begun to blaspheme. I assure you that the proprietors of these sites have no more control over what happens to your spirit or soul than does Santa Claus, the Easter Bunny and the Great Pumpkin combined. *Furthermore, **know** that authors of such statements have no exclusive link to the Divine that you don't have.* They are simply selling a cure for your fear, a symptom. Root your moral compass in compassion first. Then no 'evil spirits of any kind' can have control over your spirit or actions, regardless of your spiritual orientation.

We could examine many more examples of pure reason, pure spirituality or both, but the culminating point of the discussion is this. It is fundamentally necessary for all of Us to actively practice compassion. By embracing this reality, We come full circle with Schopenhauer's realization that, *'true morality arises in compassion'*. Now is always the best time to make compassion your passion.

STILLNESS AND ACTION

There are risks and costs to action. But they are far less than the long range risks of comfortable inaction. –John F. Kennedy, 35th American President (Lived 1917-1963)

When embarking on the enlightenment path, many people listen to great teachers and thinkers who practice the art of being still and how it opens the way of awareness. This practice is as old as recorded history, yet modern westernized civilization appears to struggle more today than in the past to slow down let alone stand still. However, We are witnessing a resurgence of interest in practicing Stillness in the western world with expansion of eastern influences in meditation, yoga, Qigong practices. In addition, modern authors such as Wayne Dyer, Deepak Chopra, Eckard Tolles and others help relate these practices to spiritual existence.

Stillness is defined as the practice of awareness in the present or the "Now" according to Eckard Tolles (96). When practiced as either a focused meditation (i.e. deliberate time allocated for such practice) or as a walking meditation (i.e. creating pockets of awareness during all aspects of your life), stillness has a powerful effect of raising ones awareness of self. By self, I don't mean the ranting voice, continually debating daily life in your mind, I mean the Universal self which is free from your chaotic thought patterns. I would encourage anyone serious about learning such practices to read works by the authors listed above. Better yet, seek out professionally trained teachers with solid references in Yogic,

Tai Chi or Qigong practices. Each type yields a slightly different experience. However, all enable extended moments of expansive stillness and oneness with something greater than the body. I emphasize, only use professionally trained teachers when dealing with your mind. Why do I say that? Would you have a doctor who didn't finish medical school or an acupuncturist that took a couple of classes at the community college work on your body? Your mind is no different and arguably even more precious.

Action is defined as the practice of 'doing' in the present. It can be expressed in many ways, such as, practicing or participating in a sport, doing work in a garden, working at the office, playing an instrument or even simply talking with a friend or family member. Without action, humanity would cease to produce anything. Populations would starve. Civilization as we know it would collapse. ***Action is the act of actualizing Our intentions.*** People would never be able to accomplish amazing feats of skill in the physical and mental Universe without both the intention of an action, followed by acting on that intention. Otherwise, intention is simply an unrealized dream of the mind.

Why are these two concepts, 'Stillness' and 'Action' so important? To answer that, let's take a closer look at how 'Stillness' and 'Action' express themselves in the human spirit. For the purpose of this discussion, We'll create two simplified categories of human mental personalities the 'Activist' and the 'Passivist'.

An 'activist' views 'reality' as the physical environment around them perceived through their logical mind. Activists have a firm belief in logic alone and typically agree with the phrase, "I'll believe it when I see it." Many people educated in western cultures fall into this category. Mathematicians, accountants, lawyers, physicians, physicists, scientists and engineers who make their trade on exercising their logical prowess tend to be activists.

Action rules the behavior and personality of activists. They constantly look for issues or problems to be acted on or solve. As a result, these individuals constantly set goals, measure where they are and review their results when completed. Serious bouts of depression, anger, guilt and doubt can arise if the results of action don't measure up to expectation or fail to appear all together. Eventually the activist recovers and instead of seeking a different path they reinvest deeper into the same path thinking,

"Next time will be better of course, so it's on to the next goal." These emotions begin to rule the *activist's* future actions whether they are warranted or not. The activist becomes a rat on a wheel, running over and over again chasing the cheese. The irony is the cheese is outside the wheel completely.

Activists exhibit a full range of behaviors from the optimistic and ambitious types to extremely pessimistic and critical types. The individual activist mind feels trapped even when between these two extremes. The driven ambitious types are trapped by the need for more, better or different for the driven ambitious types. Alternatively, the excessively pessimistic types trap themselves by their own continual, circular and hypercritical analysis of existence. They paralyze themselves into inaction. A common phrase for this behavior is *'paralysis by analysis'*, which applies to any action not just spiritual ones.

Do you see an aspect of yourself falling into this category? How do you get out of this self made prison? Let me ask this, "How do you win an argument with yourself?" The answer is don't start. Instead of blindly running to the next goal, slow down. Look around. Notice the path you are running. If and when you arrive at your destination, is the result at all what you thought it would be? Does that fundamentally change the divine connection within you? What if it didn't turn out like you planned? Will your infinite self care? Before choosing another goal, see if the *Flow* takes you elsewhere. Take time to listen to the Universe. What is your calling? Choose your next goal with care.

Passivists are the antagonists of Activist ambition. Passivists embrace the practice and power of Stillness and typically feel best when isolated and uninterrupted. The Passivist prefers to be in a constant state of awareness and not have any responsibilities or obligations to anyone or anything. They feel they are in the perpetual state of love and compassion. However, some fall into selfish indulgence with little regard for others. Pure Passivists often fail to fully contribute to the awakening Earth or Universe in concrete ways. Thus selfishness rules their existence which countermands their idea of themselves as giving.

Passivists come in a range of personalities as well. Aloof monks, who study stillness among themselves, rarely share their revelations with the masses. Imagine how much good could come from actively sharing such practice with the masses, which need illumination the most. Another personality is the lone soul that becomes so far removed from living society that they have become a personification of selfishness or self righteousness. The lone soul often suffers from a superiority complex since they rarely engage with others. The irony, from Our earlier discussions, is that We are all equally divine emerging from the Source. Even Our deepest studies in physics confirm that We are literally of the same Mind. Therefore, to think one individual is more divine or more worthy of communion with the Divine Source than another is the ego talking and not the true self.

Here is where Activists (Action Driven) and Passivists (Stillness Driven) have problems. They often discount, ignore or look on the other as inferior. Activists believe in action for anything to happen. Therefore, inaction seems implausible. Passivists believe inaction generates moral intention, imagination and creativity within Stillness of the present. Therefore, all worthwhile things fall into place naturally (96).

So who is right? The short answer is a balance of both. The following example proves the point. Your family is meditating, praying, or relaxing in the living room. Suddenly, the TV announces a hurricane is on course to devastate your town within 12 hours. The local authorities recommend everyone to evacuate. Do you refrain from moving your awareness to your logical, egocentric mind staying in bliss while the hurricane hits, or do you allow yourself to logically solve the issue at hand and move your family to safety? Most of Us, would find safety. Incidentally, in times of impending crises, monks, yogi masters and other relatively Stillness practiced people muster the wisdom to find refuge.

Before Activists get too full of themselves, let's examine the reverse case. Execution of action should be governed by compassionate wisdom that arises from the stillness within. What do I mean by that? A calm logical approach to solving the evacuation problem above is sufficient without sacrificing moral obligations. Revisiting Our hurricane family, the parents get the rest of the family and perhaps pets to safety before them. Logically the parents know they probably would run faster, carry less and get to safety more easily. However, their sense of morality, compassion and love motivates them to help the family as a whole, regardless of increased risk or time of departure. Any other action is seen as fundamentally immoral and cowardly. Likewise, refusing to decide to act and commit to non-action would be considered negligent at minimum and completely irresponsible with respect to the children. It may be understandable to accept your own fate. It is not acceptable to impose your fate on others, particularly the innocent who rely on you.

In summary, people need to learn to use their moral compassion and intention, emerging from Stillness practice, to guide their Actions. Then simply have the courage to act. This vital balance is integral to stay on Our individual paths and to survive as a species.

Insight #22: From Stillness comes Compassion to guide Action

Interestingly, experimental evidence shows the practice of Stillness (i.e. mediation) increases compassion in the form of, empathy (94). A research study, sponsored by the National Institutes of Health-National Center for Complementary and Alternative Medicine (NCCAM), performed at the University of Wisconsin, used functional Magnetic Resonance Imaging (fMRI) to compare brain images of 16 expert meditators to 16 novice meditators. The study found that the expert meditators showed a measurable increase brain activity in areas of the brain associated with empathy not found among the novices. The researchers concluded that there was a real, measureable increase in empathy capacity among expert meditators versus novice meditators.

What does this study and others suggest to the greater populace? If empathy is the seed that springs compassion, and compassion defines humanity's moral compass, perhaps the global society should embrace and practice a bit more Stillness before taking action. Therefore, once the way to action is revealed, and logically implemented, move boldly forward, keeping an eye on compassion. This way we use compassion as our source and compass for all actions. The goal behind this method is to prevent Us from undermining or destroying the very fabric of greater good We are trying to achieve. Practically speaking, the 'Compassion-to-Action' process should be accomplished while minimizing the introduction of bias noise from politics, institutional and religious dogma. Remember, there is no power standing between Us and the Divine Source. The illusion of that power is only created if given. It is never taken.

CHAPTER 9
THE WAY FORWARD

-If science proves some belief of Buddhism wrong, then Buddhism will have to change. In my view, science and Buddhism share a search for the truth and for understanding reality. By learning from science about aspects of reality where its understanding may be more advanced, I believe that Buddhism enriches its own worldview-

-Tenzin Gyatso, 14th Dalai Lama

SPIRITUAL EVOLUTION: THE CORE PATH

In this Chapter, We introduce the centered path or 'Core' path representing a change in traditional western and eastern views of the Universe. For this change to occur, anyone who wishes to spiritually evolve must have the <u>will</u> and <u>courage</u> to do so even in the midst of resistance. Thus, the volition to act and be that change is encapsulated in the coined phrase 'Spiritual Evolution'.

Traditionally, *The Way* is an ancient term for '*the path*' or *journey* of enlightenment. However, when reductionist scientific methods entered into the philosophical discussion, most religions around the world resisted this perceived new threat. Science was a new form of noetic knowledge gathering. It placed evidence and logic above hearsay, and began displacing long standing dogma. Established world religions at the time had foundations based on the institution interpreting matters of nature and spirit. Suddenly, matters of nature were being taken away from them. Similarly, noetic spiritual practices of enlightenment without a structured hierarchy such as,

'The Way' of the Taoists were also seen as a threat to the three main monotheistic religions. Therefore, Buddhism, Hinduism, Taoism and others were seen as heretical in the eyes of the Christianity, Islam and Judaism. Such ideas probably hindered eastern philosophy expansion for centuries. More recently, globalization and the internet created interconnectedness across humanity never before seen. With this increased connectedness, 'The Path' has reemerged in the consciousness of many westernized minds, yet the value of science cannot be ignored. Therefore, the 'Core Path' is born

A simple yet generalized Venn diagram (shown in Figure 9) forms visual guide to the *Core Path*. The Venn diagram illustrates a balance which leads to a highly inspired life of spiritual existence without falling off your path. This balance is particularly important in the presence of deceptive people or institutions who would profit or gain power by unbalancing you.

The circles represent the three realms of human existence; Stillness, Thought and Action. Stillness is Our definition of pure awareness or consciousness described in Chapter 7. In this realm, spiritualism practice gives rise to joy, bliss and profound connectedness. Action is the physical doing or active participation in the physical Universe. In this realm, science flourishes and modern physics promotes theories and provides evidence for describing the quantum and relativistic Universe. Thought is what is typically referred to as the thinking mind. This realm is where We ponder, calculate and internally dialog, as I am doing right now while committing these words to the page.

At the intersections of any two realms of existence, three guiding, yet powerful, principles surround the Core Path; Compassion, Inspiration and Intention. All three arise from blending the three primary realms of human existence.

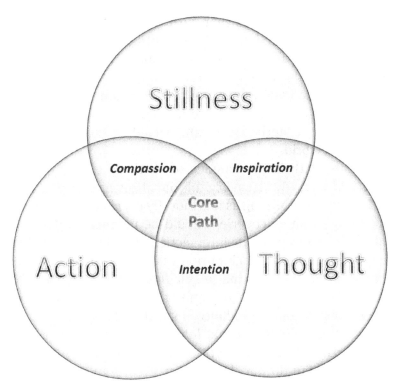

Figure 9: the Core Path Venn diagram for modern human spiritual experience. The realms of human existence are within Stillness, Action and Thought. The intersections generate interactions between each realm of existence giving rise to the principles: Compassion, Inspiration and Intention. The intersection of all three principles is a modern path of enlightenment, the 'Core Path'.

Compassion is the Action that arises from Stillness previously discussed in scientific studies (94). *Inspiration* arises from Stillness to Thought. It come in many forms among them imagination, creativity and motivation. This explains why *inspiration* requires an intuitive leap particularly in the arts and sciences. *Inspiration* is the true inception of new ideas and creative thought, which when motivated can also be contagious. Think of a wondrous piece of music, beautiful artwork, or amazing invention. Usually, they have come about from such inspired sources as nature or dreams. Finally, *intention* is the crossover of thought with the volition to act. *Intention* can take on many forms. One form is emotional thoughts leading to action. Emotional intentions can reap great rewards when channeled properly or disastrous results if not understood.

This is the primary reason that most 'self-help' experts focus on this one area. However, it misses all the other factors of a balanced existence. Another form of *intention* is focused and often logical. This form of *intention* is well practiced by those trained in the sciences or mathematics, since often there are long periods of focus in the realm of thought to create intended actions on the other end. The scientific method is a standard aid for this process in the experimental world.

The Core Path is the balance of all three circles of human existence. Inspired discovery of our Universe uses modern scientific intention as long as it is morally checked by compassion. Of course all such discoveries should be independently verified and debate encouraged. The intersection of Stillness, Thought and Action creates an equilibrium point required to conduct, learn and incorporate new information via *Integrative Science or (IS)*. IS represents a serious effort to reunite the power of scientific rigor with the compassionate guidance of spirituality.

I don't mean to suggest that *Integrative Science* is not already being performed by some practitioners, but for those professional practitioners who do not, *Integrative Science* gives professional practitioners a personal and institutional compass with which to grow, a reconnection of purpose with reason without the traditional burdens of religious doctrine or limiting scope of pure materialism science. Ironically, many famous scientists are integrative scientists. Einstein, Schrödinger and Bose all had definite purpose behind their inquiries and were very spiritual people. The popular disconnected belief promoted by some atheists reveals an illusory separation (26). In truth, perpetuating such a facade opens the flood gates to ignorance and wild speculation particularly from fundamentalist groups (97).

Although anyone can participate in personal transformative practice of the Core Path, I am not condoning wholesale spiritual research without a healthy dose of honest skepticism, rigor and debate. **Professional *Integrative Science*, as a discipline, must maintain high levels of integrity, undergo independent review, have mass observable results and be openly and vigorously debated.** This path is the only way to prevent religious doctrine, external pressures or academic dogma to rule the direction and scope of inspirational investigation. As in materialism science, the results of theory, experimentation along with the governance by compassion are the guiding factors for future investigations. Thus the Integrative Scientist is also a practitioner of the Core Path.

People on both sides of the fence argue for keeping science out of religion and religion out of science. I tend to agree on this point. Powerful special interests can particularly twist religion or science institutions. Wealthy and influential companies, institutions and politicians who feel their brand of truth is 'Too big to fail' try to affect outcomes so that they can continue to promote their own dogma above all else. However, as humanity is faced with global level issues that require billions of Us to work together to solve, We need fresh approaches and perspectives.

Integrative Science, devoid of past prejudices, dogmatic biases, favoritism and blame, is an emerging phenomenon by practice although not by name. Therefore, the Core Path stands for a logical, spiritually balanced and guided existence, as well as, a blueprint toward modern spiritual growth. The approach can solve issues ranging from localized social outbreaks of hate crimes to Our largest scientific and philosophical quandaries of the 21st Century.

- Who are We?

- Why are We here?

- What is Our purpose?

- What is Earth's purpose?

- How do We live at peace and balance with each other and with Earth?

- How do We fit into the Universe?

- What is the nature of the Divine Source?

- Since We are an integral part of the Divine Source, what should We, as a whole, be doing to promote the progress of life on Earth?

- How do We grow civilization without destroying the very life giving planet that We are a part of?

- What happens after We pass on?

- Is there life after death?

- If so, what kind?

- Where are We going?

REDEFINING OUR PLACE IN THE UNIVERSE

If humanity applies scientific logic and action mediated by stillness (meditative) practice, We begin to move away from selfishness. Instead of generating systemic problems within ourselves and surrounding environment, We begin creating solutions which preserve Our relatedness with each other, Nature and the Universe as a whole. The sooner We begin acting like stewards of all of Nature, the quicker We begin providing for the future of all life on this planet.

My next book in the Evolution Series will take a serious look at how to expand personal worldview ideas and apply them toward greater integration with the world. This mergence creates an Integrative Science environment at a global scale to help humanity shape scientific policy, the decision making process and realization to better the whole planet. As We discovered in Chapter 5, when groups, especially large groups, of human minds focus on a task or event, dramatic quantum level affects start reshaping the order of the Universe around Us. If We learn to channel this group effect in productive rather than destructive ways, We will change the direction of humanity from 'selfish destruction' to 'collaborative production'.

Throughout this book, We have discovered evidence supporting that We indeed are part of the collective universal consciousness. Furthermore, We are inseparable from the ultimate complex adaptive system, the Universe; and thus, have universal modeling capability contained within each and every one of Us. Human minds teeter on a complex, chaotic border between order and disorder giving Us no defined boundary. Thus the possibilities are truly endless.

Physiological study concludes that Our conscious selves are made up of living and non-living components. Quantum physics information research suggests, at the level of the cosmos, a universally conscious system is indeed the superset of all sentient life. Therefore, it is not unreasonable to propose the following theory. ***The entirety of the system, the Universal 'Mind', is living.*** This theory is similar to the 'God Theory' proposed by physicist Bernard Haisch (54). He and his colleagues create a model of the Zero-Point Field inertia hypothesis which is compatible with a manifestation of the 'Mind' of God. Haisch and colleagues' theoretical model reportedly accounts for the major relativistic laws, such as the limiting speed for any mass as the speed of light. Haisch accomplishes this by suggesting that all particles in the known Universe, people included, exist in the Zero-Point field of energy which is analogous to absolute zero when measuring temperature.

The Zero-Point field is the lowest energetic state that has existed since the dawn of time. Perhaps even before the Big Bang if Sir Roger Penrose's claims are correct (98). Sir Penrose believes that the circular patterns shown in the cosmic microwave background (Figure 10 below), a representation of the lowest energy levels across the known Universe, suggest that there is no Big Bang, but instead "cycles through a series of '*aeons*'." The Zero-point energy field is observable through these universal background radiation measurements and detectible pressure forces between to infinitesimally spaced plates known as Casimir forces.

Figure 10: Data collected over seven years by NASA's Wilkinson Microwave Anisotropy Probe (WMAP) Satellite. (Courtesy of NASA.)

Haisch uses Zero-Point field physics to develop an argument for the *manifest* God, or directly knowable God. The manifest God means that God, or Source referenced here, *is* knowable because Source is in constant direct contact with all things at all times. Source *is* the knowable Universe (54). At first blush, Haisch and colleagues' theory challenges the idea of a God limited by physical laws presented in Stephen Hawking and Leonard Mlodinow's book, "The Grand Design" (55).

Hawking and Mlodinow write, with regard to physical laws, *"Because there is a law such as gravity, the Universe can and will create itself from nothing. Spontaneous creation is the reason there is something rather than nothing, why the Universe exists, why We exist."* Another excerpt from their book states, *"It is not necessary to invoke God to light the blue touch paper and set the Universe going."* This assumption presumes a *non-manifest* (unknowable) God that exists external to the Universe.

Let's compare these ideas and look at what's being said. Haisch's model suggests the 'manifest God' is the Source of all matter and therefore it would be implausible since any matter would have to include mass, and thus be subject to all laws limiting mass such as relativity, inertia and conservation. This argument is similar to what Hawking and Mlodinow say except in different words. Therefore, it makes sense that the idea of an all omnipotent being made purely of its own laws and matter appears redundant. Which came first, Source or the Cosmic Egg or are we asking the wrong question?

We could alternatively argue, as Haisch does, that We and the Universe are products of the *'unmanifest'* Divine Source or a "God Beyond Matter" or 'supermatter', but then the circular question haunts Us. Who made the Source? Hawking and Mlodinow's statement above, that **"the Universe can and will create itself from nothing"** is based on modern cosmic and quantum models along with experimentation. Haisch and most physicists are in agreement on this, which then gives rise to the question, "Is God redundant? If so, why is there redundancy in God? If not, where is or perhaps the better question what is God?"

Haisch suggests this answer

> *"...the Universe, in its full temporal evolution, is the all-at-once ideation of God. I submit that creation is not an over-and-done*

*thing; the present and future existence of the Universe is as much
an act of creation as what We call the 'beginning.' Creation did
not happen; it is. Moreover, I propose that the continuous flow
of light energy in the form of the zero-point field of the quantum
vacuum—in whose reference frame there is also no extension in
space and time—may be the mechanism for this ongoing creation.
The question, from a scientific perspective, becomes: Can the
quantum fluctuations of the zero-point field be the agents that
make matter stable and make things happen at the atomic level?"*

Haisch's model is in agreement with the model derived in this book using the sciences of emergence, information and complexity. If information is truly massless, then it exists all the way down to the zero-point field, at Planck's scale. Here information is not impaired by relativity, space or time and can travel in entangled, non-local causal networks.

This concept implies that inception of ideas can come from virtually anywhere or anytime. Also, the 'existence' of the informational God 'Mind' is present at all times, and spaces. Therefore, the manifest 'Body of God' (i.e. the physical Universe) would not be a static system, but rather, a dynamic, ever evolving, and complex system. The 'Body of God' would have a 'birth' via the Big Bang Theory or Big Bounce Theory, which minimizes radius, information and energy while maximizing mass. The 'Body of God' would also have a 'death' via all mass dissolving into energy and increased entropy to nothing or achieving a maximum radius, information and energy and minimum mass only to reverse again.

Both of these Universe scenarios are hotly debated among physicists. The reason for the debate is that the jury is still out on the evidence for the physical beginning and ending of Our Universe. Perhaps the Universe is cyclical in nature as many physicists and scientists such as Randal Mills and Sir Roger Penrose believe and has no end (48) (98). This idea only holds water if We can account for enough mass in the system to allow the accelerating stellar bodies to decelerate and collapse. If We cannot find enough mass, then the Universe would fade to pure entropy and information. From this pure energetic, informational state, another Big Bang event within the 'Source Mind' would be required to initiate a new Universe or 'Source Body'. Notice, however, in either scenario information remains, its form changes. In addition, the philosophy of reincarnation at the astronomical scale is suggested and plausible. This is the ultimate in recycling programs!

So in answer to Hawking and Mlodinow's assertion that God is redundant, my answer is of course it is! It is no stranger a thought than the inherent belief that Our minds, defined by Our thoughts, are parallel to and redundant with the physical brain. However, the interplay between the two in human existence allows the mind to create and receive information which allows Us to model and interpret what Our body is experiencing. Could the same be true for a Universal consciousness or *'Divine Source Mind'* that interacts with and is parallel with the physical Universe or *'Source Body'*? If so, what do We know of that could account for such a parallel?

One such theory lies in quantum information transfer. Faster than light (FTL) information transfer is being examined across the globe in devices from quantum entanglement key transfer to superluminal devices and may provide the foundation for a non-local causal informational network (50) (73) (76) (77) (99). Such informational science research may in fact lead humankind to ultimately discover the mechanisms behind the 'Mind' of the Universe.

Whether or not Mills, Haisch, Hawking or others have the best physics model of the Universe, the mere presence of Our conscious selves in this Universe implies that parallel Body and Mind existence naturally occurs and is feasible. If all conscious entities everywhere are agents of this emergent 'Mind' of the Divine Source or 'God-Mind' then there should be some evidence to them being interconnected by means other than chemical, physical or via some electromagnetic field that is limited by relativity. Interestingly there is. Studies proving this idea have been done for decades in the field of psi studies. A compelling study performed in 1994 was published in the Physics Essays Journal (100). In the study, pairs of people that were allowed to interact for twenty minutes via meditation were isolated in enclosed sound proof, Faraday rooms, meaning that all forms of physical communication, auditory and electromagnetic information transfer would be blocked. Subject A was stimulated by light flashes to their eyes which show up in averaged brain signals while subject B sits silently in an isolated chamber. The study found that ~25% of the pairs that underwent this "entanglement" interaction would see the stimulated brain signal in subject B even though their brain was not being stimulated. Furthermore, control groups showed that without previous interaction between the subjects, no correlation between their brain signals were evident. There may be a logical explanation for this 25% success rate figure between the pairs, one sender and one receiver. A possible explanation could be that human minds are predisposed to send or receive quantum information. If this is the case and assuming a 50:50 chance of being a sender or receiver, the possible combinations of a pair of individuals are the following:

- Sender → Sender
- Sender → Receiver
- Receiver → Sender
- Receiver → Receiver

Notice the only combination that may yield a strong enough measurable evoked potential would be the Sender→Receiver case, which would be 25% of the time. If this phenomenon were taken into account, it would be prudent to reexamine previous psi studies requiring a sender and receiver and look for this 25% deviation. I suspect that the increases seen in Ganzfield experiments, remote viewing and studies on the sense of being stared at will deviate from chance by ~25% +/- some deviation. Furthermore, if the above study could be used as a precursor for identifying participants as either a sender or receiver, then some of the classical studies of psi phenomenon could be revisited by, using matched pairs to see if the odds against chance increase to create a somewhat reliable quantum communications link between people. Currently researchers are working on trying to create quantum explanations for this 'entangled mind' phenomenon (101).

This *integrative informational model* also complies with emergence theory for complex adaptive systems of multiple scales. A parallel physical-informational coexistence also raises an interesting question. If the Divine Source has this dualistic nature of eternal (Mind) and non-eternal or cyclical (Body), are We and all life created from the same characteristics as the Universal body and mind? It seems logical and plausible. If so, Our 'minds' are informationally linked to the One eternal 'Mind' and thus; this element of Our nature is truly eternal. Therefore, the dualistic nature of Source and sentient life *has* redundancy by definition. Recognition of this redundancy has been part of ancient philosophy, particularly in Eastern Indian and Taoist culture, since the dawn of civilization. Thus, even the Universe, Divine Source, has the character of both birth and death while keeping the essence of Life, eternal.

In fact, most robust complex adaptive systems we know of rely on multiple redundancies at various levels of scale. These redundancies allow a system, like the human body, Earth or the world economy, to extend its existence for much longer than it would otherwise last. We have different names for these redundant systems depending upon the system. In the human body for example the nervous and endocrine feedback control systems redundantly and synergistically control body factors such as blood pH and pressure, hormone and temperature levels and heart rate.

Insight # 23: Humankind's imagination of Source is limited. Source's imagination of humankind is not.

Reexamine the human *Core Path* diagram, Figure 9, above. Superimpose a universal informational network, interconnecting all systems at all levels of scale in the Universe. We create an admittedly simplistic yet elegantly refined diagram showing human existence in relation to the Universe (See Figure 11 below). This revised diagram adds the possibility for interactions with the Universal Informational Network (UIN) or 'God-mind', as integral to human experience, since human experience is a subset of the global system. This is an admittedly crude representation of the theory that I am presenting; however, it serves as a visual to spark a larger conversation for those not directly at the cutting edge of quantum research. Hypothetically, it may turn out that UIN operates at several levels of scale. In the book, *Code of God: The Spiritual Odyssey of a Man of Science*, physicist Mani Bhaumik suggests instant connections may occur at the quantum field level of scale and perhaps even smaller near Planck's scale from what physicists, such as David Bohm and others, call the Prime Field (102). This Prime Field is postulated to be the fabric of potentiality, the founding consciousness for the rest of the physical fields such as the gravity field and electromagnetic field that we have verified. Rupert Sheldrake hypothesizes a similar idea of a 'Morphogenetic Field' that gives rise to all of natures forms and retains a memory of past forms (103). Regardless if there are one or more scales of informational transfer, we model the whole as a Universal Information Network.

Through awareness practices in stillness, We calm Our actions and thoughts and experience the sense of being 'connected'. Thus it seems highly likely that Our best bet for experiencing universal connectedness is when we are still, unclouded by physical and mental stressors.

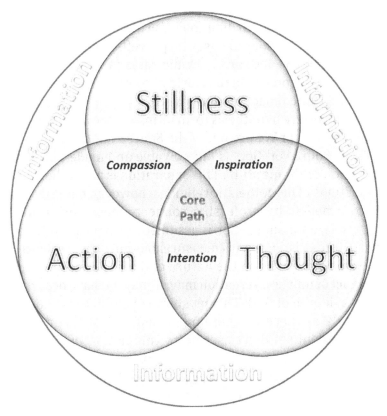

Figure 11: Revised Core Path diagram for modern human spiritual experience including the Universal Informational Network (UIN).

How does profound connectedness occur in everyday experience? It comes in the form of quiet inspiration as you listen to a song, study a painting or experience an epiphany. Perhaps a powerful connection presents itself by waking you in the middle of the night to a sudden solution to a mathematical or scientific problem. Profound connectedness even occurs through the simple act of compassion for someone or something that otherwise would go unnoticed.

Some communications through the UIN are less about connecting with the whole and more about connecting to others within the network. An agonizing feeling that your brother, sister or other family member is in trouble and you subsequently call only to find out it is so. Many such cases are reported and directly experienced by many of Us, myself included (45) (101). In addition, evidence points to people capable of transmitting information in unexplainable ways according to classical physics (79) (100). For instance, groups of people focused on peaceful meditation or prayer show observable reductions in crime rates (45). Many additional unexplained phenomena in the world become explainable if We can understand Our connection with the UIN.

The alternative hypothesis to an intimate, knowable connection with Source is that We are not *of* the Source but objectively made by it. Thus Source or 'God' is unknowable and made of a different composition of 'divine stuff'. This separation is an implied belief in many factions of monotheistic religions; however, many contradict their own beliefs by professing connectedness with God. If an unknowable, un-manifest God is assumed and it purely initiates the Universe into existence with measureable rules, then science truly has no answers for Us on the nature of God. Therefore, outside of how the act of universal creation may or may not have occurred, We have no evidence of God. This mystery is behind the fundamental question, "Was there a beginning or end?" Most theoretical and empirical scientists don't ascribe to this notion of God since, if Source is not part of the knowable Universe, then We can only speculate about God. We resign ourselves to understanding the initial conditions, if any, of the Universe and the rules which We can know.

Interestingly, Stephen Hawking has caused quite a stir with religious groups around the world with this very viewpoint (104) (105). Hawking does not believe in heaven or un-manifest external God. He does however believe in a manifest possibility. Quoting from an interview with Diane Sawyer:

"What could define God [is a conception of divinity] as the embodiment of the laws of nature. However, this is not what most people would think of that God... They made a human-like being with which one can have a personal relationship. When you look at the vast size of the universe and how insignificant an accidental human life is in it that seems most impossible."

In the separate un-manifest case where God is truly unknowable, why would it care what happened to us? Furthermore, any such connection, by anyone in this universe to such a being would be false by definition and the Universe would be an awful waste of space. I subscribe that this is counter to nature, because if there is anything that nature has taught Us, it's that nature wastes nothing.

THE WAY BEYOND

-We are all one and We shall be again.-

Astrophysicist Stephen Hawking believes that, *"I regard the brain as a computer which will stop working when its components fail. There is no heaven or afterlife for broken down computers; that is a fairy story for people afraid of the dark..."* (105).

Other eminent scientists are working on getting evidence to prove otherwise by trying to answer questions like. What happens when Our transient bodies die? Do We just fade away or do We exist in some other form?

Psychologists, medical doctors and neuroscientists in particular are at the forefront of answering these previously taboo questions. Thus far, there is suggestive evidence and case studies of something tangible happening at or near death, but the exact nature is unclear. I should pause this discussion to warn you. When looking up information on these topics, the internet is arguably one of the largest sources of misinformation in existence. Please, review reputable studies being conducted. Even then, look for independent verification from other reliable sources.

Using the above criterion as an initial guide, some evidence from early studies suggested that there is perhaps mass to Our 'souls' or spirits which can be measured when We die, but more meticulous research is required for validation. (106) The most often misquoted and infamous of these experiments was performed by Duncan

MacDougall in 1921. He took it upon himself to weigh 6 people as they were dying and reported that the body lost an average of 21 grams based upon 4 of the 6 bodies. Deeper examination of his data reveals that it actually ranged from 11 to 43 grams and it is unclear why some souls would weigh more or less than others.

It turns out that these studies were not repeatable by others and the apparent soul weight could be accounted for by more materialistic explanations such as evaporation of water and expiration of gases in the body. However, further attempts to improve on the experiment are being pursued by Gerard Nahum, a physician and director of medical affairs at Berlex (formerly of Duke University's School of Medicine). He argues that a repeat of the experiment is possible to control for such variables. In principle the experiment would have an extremely sensitive mass scale, a spherical array of electromagnetic (EM) detectors to pick up energy ranging from low energy microwaves on up to gamma rays and surround that with an EM containment shield (Faraday Cage) to eliminate outside interference.

The theory, according to Nahum, is that "all of what's embodied in it (the soul, spirit or essence) cannot just simply disappear. It needs to either be transformed into something else with Our space-time, or it needs to transcend its existence here and move on to someplace else where it could potentially remain intact." Although Nahum has proposed this to many groups and universities within the United States, they have not yet taken up the mantle. Perhaps the parallel quantum information network is our collective essence that continues on?

Note: there are falsified articles on the web on this topic. For example, www.noeticsciences.co.uk , which claims that a study published in an East German Journal Horizon, by Dr. Becker Mertens of Dresden and Dr. Elke Fisher successfully weighed the souls of some 200 terminally ill patients resulting in a weight of 1/3000th of an ounce. I and others have investigated the matter and can find no such Dr. Becker or Dr. Fisher in East Germany associated with Dresden, and no Horizon East German journal. This type of miss information is a growing problem, especially for people overly reliant upon the web for information. Such irresponsible fabrication does not serve the scientific community or general public.

In contrast, credible work has been done in neuroscience regarding Out of Body Experiences or (OBEs). Neuroscientist, Olaf Blanke at Swiss Federal Institute of Technology in Lausanne, studies inducing the OBE by stimulating the temporal-parietal junction (typically used for body orientation). Dr. Blanke, was able to induce this out of body experience in an awakened female patient. Dr. Blanke told Discover Magazine, *"While we were stimulating it, she was awake and not impaired in any sense, and she told us that she saw the world, including us three investigators and herself lying on the bed, from this elevated perspective."* While the above is argued by Blanke to be a neurological illusion and does not necessarily prove the separation of a spirit from the body it does provide an opening, a tool to use to better understand the OBEs (106) (107). Perhaps stimulus of this part of the brain triggers a naturally occurring response during death?

Related to OBDs are Near Death Experiences or (NDE)s. There are a surprising number of cases where the OBD neural experience above fails to account for the experience. Chris Carter, author of the book, *"Science and the Near-Death Experience: How Consciousness Survives Death,"* covers many of these case studies in detail (108). The book effectively refutes stimulated physiological, pharmacological and psychological explanations of NDEs. Of particular interest are cases where the patient's are blind and clinically dead. These states prohibit the previous stimulated neuroscience argument since a patient cannot see through their eyes normally, yet reported being able to "see" objects in the room. Furthermore, some patients described events in the operating room (OR) that they could have not directly perceived and the physicians did not discuss (109). One particular documented example highlighted in the National Geographic documentary, *Moment of Death*. A man clinically died during a surgical procedure that required his eyes to be covered. Upon resuscitation, this same patient reported he was looking down from above the surgical table off to the side near the ceiling seeing the surgeons working on his body. He further elaborated that his surgeon was doing a 'chicken dance' in the OR. After awakening from surgery, the man asked the surgeon what the 'chicken dance' was for. The surgeon had not told the patient that during long surgeries, he would stretch his back and loosen up by folding his arms in (to keep his hands sterile) and twist and turn.

The surgeon wanted to know how he knew, since it was impossible for the patient to see the surgeon because his eyes were covered during the surgery.

Stuart Hameroff and Roger Penrose's work on the interaction of microtubules with quantum level events, explored earlier in Chapter 5, suggests a counter hypothesis (80). Hameroff commented in regards to the possibility of an 'entangled functional unit' that suggests a continuation of consciousness. Here are some excerpts of Hameroff's statements (106):

> *"I think consciousness under normal circumstances occurs at the level of space-time geometry in the brain, in the microtubules..." "...But the fluctuations extend down to the Planck scale [far smaller than an atom] because the microtubules are driven bioenergetically to be in a coherent state. When the blood supply and the oxygen stops, things go bad and the coherence stops, but quantum information at the Planck scale is not lost. It may dissipate into the Universe but remain somehow entangled in some kind of functional unit, maybe indefinitely...you get patterns at the Planck scale that are constantly evolving and changing. This is where Penrose says the noncomputable influences are embedded. Even though they're very, very tiny, they repeat everywhere...If a patient is not revived," Hameroff says, "it enters the Universe at large, and maybe it gets picked back up again by someone someday, who knows?"*

Recently deceased Psychiatrist and physician Ian Stevenson, author of *Twenty Cases Suggestive of Reincarnation*, founded the Division of Perceptual Studies (DOPS) (110). Jim B. Tucker, his protégé, child psychiatrist and author of *Life Before Life: A Scientific Investigation of Children's Memories of Previous Lives* built a database of ~1,400 cases (as of 2007) of possible reincarnation (111). In an interview, Tucker suggests that the best cases usually coincide with the younger children that begin talking about what they 'used to do' (106). Tucker told Discover Magazine that, *"Kids tend to start talking about these memories at an earlier age. They talk about them with more emotion. They give a lot of details; including specific names about the previous life....We would never say that we have proved that reincarnation occurs. I think we can only say that we've produced evidence for it."* I encourage you to read the case studies for yourself and draw your own conclusions.

So when asking, why are We here? What becomes of Us? How do I connect with Source? What can We glean from Our travels through this book and will such information answer some of these questions? The simple act of asking why *is* the Core Path. To be able to ask why may be the simple answer.

We know through direct experience and now Our science that We are integral players in the Universe. Therefore, Our actions are governed not just by laws of the land, but greater scientific and moral laws of existence. Action governed by compassion places Us in alignment with the Source. Without Our moral compass arising from compassion, We and those We love and care about loose out.

As for what's next, The Core Path *is* where eternal life exists. It exists every moment We revel in nature's beauty, act from compassion and meditate in silence. When people ask, "what happens when I die," they are really asking, "what happens to my ego, my identity." If We assume the ego is the logical and emotional mind with a fragile story about its identity, it is not necessarily required for the eternal living part. Or perhaps it gets encoded on some form of informational dynamic memory in the UIN. If the later approaches the truth, then We could envision the 'soul' or 'spirit' as existing beyond the body in the UIN. The soul would literally exist as dynamic information that may possibly be able to interact with other information and matter.

Emerging evidence shows that something profound is happening at the time of the death of the body, but more work needs to be done in this area (108). Eckhart Tolle, in the Zen Buddhist tradition, claims that the eternal living part of you is the observer of your thoughts and emotions, and that this part of you is the actual YOU (96). In other words, ***You are eternal life***. This resonates when We examine the literal Hebrew word for soul, *nephesh*, which literally translates to ***life or vital breath***.

As for why do We have Our bodies? Experiences teach Us, catastrophes humble Us, tragedy generates compassion within Us and everyday miracles inspire Us. For an eternal consciousness, these emotional understandings may require noetic knowledge and thus the necessity of fragile, transient forms, such as the human body.

On the question of communion with the Source, We discover the final insight through Our journey in this book.

Insight #24: We are always connected to Source, but not always directing attention to it.

All We know is that We are undoubtedly physically, causally and informationally linked with Our Planet and Universe. The nature, number and speed of these links are still being tested, probed and studied by multitudes of scientists across the globe with various backgrounds. What is true is Our internal Universe and Our external Universe are ultimately ***One***.

WORKS CITED

1. **Griffin, Jasper, Boardman, John and Murray, Oswyn.** *The Oxford history of Greece and the Hellenistic world.* Oxford : Oxford University Press, 2001. ISBN 0-19-280137-6.

2. **Kirsch, Jonathan.** *God Against the Gods: The History of the War Between Monotheism and Polytheism.* New York : Viking Compass, 2004. 978-0670032860.

3. **Ginzburg, Carlo.** *The Cheese and the Worms: The Cosmos of a Sixteenth Century Miller.* Baltimore : Johns Hopkins University Press, 1980. ISBN 0-8018-4387-1.

4. **di Vito, mancuso.** Intolleranza Religiosa- Alle Radici Della Violenza. *Panorama.it.* [Online] 11 14, 2006. [Cited: October 20, 2010.] http://archivio.panorama.it/home/articolo/idA020001038812.

5. **Kirsch, Johnathan.** *The Grand Inquisitor's Manual: A history of Terror in the Name of God.* New York : Harper One, 2008. 978-0060816995.

6. **Robinson, B. A.** Levels of belief coercion within religious groups. Real & imaginary high-demand religious groups. *Religious Tolerance.org.* [Online] Aug 30, 2008. [Cited: October 21, 2010.] www.religioustolarance.org.

7. **Kuhn, Tomas.** *The Copernican Revolution.* s.l. : MJF Books, Original Copyright 1957, reprinted in 1997. 978-1567312171.

8. Ptolemaic System. *The Galileo Project.* [Online] Aug 04, 2003. [Cited: Jan 2, 2010.] http://galileo.rice.edu/sci/theories/ptolemaic_system.html.

9. **Russel, Bertrand.** *Religion and Science.* New York : Oxford University Press USA, New Ed. 1997. 978-0195115512.

10. **Heilbron, John L.** *Censorship of Astronomy in Italy after Galileo.* Notre Dame : University of Notre Dame Press, 2005. 0-268-03483-4.

11. **Sungenis, Robert.** CAI's Science Creed. [Online] Catholic Aplogetics International, None specified. [Cited: October 22, 2010.] http://www.catholicintl.com/epologetics/articles/science/scicreed.htm.

12. **Sungenis, Robert and Bennett, Robert.** *Galileo Was Wrong The Church Was Right: The Scientific Evidence for Geocentrism.* s.l. : CAI Publishing, 2010. 978-0-9841859-6-2.

13. **Bureau of Democracy, Human Rights, and Labor.** *Annual Report on International Religious Freedom.* Washington DC : United States Depart of State, 2009.

14. **National Geographic and IBM.** The Genographic Project. *National Geographic.* [Online] National Geographic and IBM, 1996-2010. [Cited: Nov 3, 2010.] https://genographic.nationalgeographic.com/genographic/lan/en/atlas.html.

15. **Potts, Richard and Sloan, Chris.** Being Human Becoming Human: Survival of the Adaptible. *What does it mean to be human?* Washington D.C. : Smithsonian Institute: The National Museum of Natural History, 2010.

16. **Society for Neuroscience.** Research & Discoveries. *Society for Neuroscience: Advancing the Understanding of the Brain and Nervous System.* [Online] 2010. [Cited: November 4, 2010.] http://www.sfn.org/skins/main/pdf/rd/alzheimers_disease.pdf.

17. [Online]

18. **Plass, Ewald M.** *What Luther Says: An Anthology.* St. Louis : Concordia Publishing House, 1959. p. 2:964.

19. **Fahlbusch, Erwin and Bromiley, Geoffrey William.** The Encyclopedia of Christianity, Vol 4. [book auth.] Erwin Fahlbusch, Jan Milic Lochman and John Mbiti. *The Encyclopedia of Christianity.* Grand Rapids, MI : William B. Eerdmans Publishing Company, 2005, p. 1:244.

20. **Shayler, David.** *Skylab: America's space station.* London, New York : Springer-Praxis, 2001. pp. 313-314. 9781852334079.

21. **Adam, John.** Case Study: "Honour Killings and Blood Feuds". *www.gendercide.org.* [Online] Gendercide Watch, 2008. [Cited: Feb. 16, 2010.] http://www.gendercide.org/case_honour.html.

22. **Gonzales, Laurence.** Mob Mentality. *National Geographic Adventure.* October, 2008, Vol. 10, 8, pp. p28-30.

23. **Singer, Peter.** *Ethics.* Oxford : Oxford University Press, 1994. 9780192892454.

24. *Oxytocin Modulates Neural Circuitry for Social Cognition and Fear in Humans.* **Kirsch, Peter, et al.** 49, s.l. : The Journal of Neuroscience, 2005, Vol. 25.

25. **BBC NEWS.** Rwanda: How the genocide happened. *BBC NEWS:World:Africa:.* [Online] 12 17, 2008. [Cited: 11 17, 2010.] http://newsvote.bbc.co.uk/go/pr/fr/-/2/hi/africa/1288230.stm.

26. **Hitchens, Christopher.** *god is not Great: How Religion Poisons Everything.* New York : Twelve Books, Hachette Book Group, 2007. 978-0446579803.

27. **Gibson, James.** Miller-McCune:Politics Religion and Intolerance in Contemporary American Politics. *Miller-McCune.* [Online] March 2, 2009. [Cited: Nov 17, 2010.] http://www.miller-mccune.com/politics/religion-and-intolerance-in-contemporary-american-politics-3916/.

28. **Shirouzu, Norihiko.** Train Makers Rail Against China's High Speed Designs. *The Wall Street Journal.* November 17, 2010.

29. **Helden, Albert Van.** *Sidereus Nuncius, or The Sidereal Messenger.* Chicago : University of Chicago Press, 1989. 978-0226279039.

30. **Stark, Rodney.** False Conflict: Christianity Is Not Only Compatible with Science—It Created It. *The American Enterprise.* October-November, 2003.

31. **Russell, Jeffrey Burton.** *Inventing the Flat Earth Columbus and Modern Historians.* New York : Praeger Paperback, 1997. 978-0275959043.

32. Nan'in Zen Master. *The Living Workshop Zen Masters.* [Online] [Cited: Nov 24, 2010.] http://www.livingworkshop.net/nanin.html.

33. **O'Conner, Zena.** Colour harmony revisited. *Color Research and Application.* August, 2010, Vol. 35, 4.

34. **Berzin, Alexander.** Handling Fear. *The Berzin Archives.* [Online] March 202. [Cited: June 21, 2010.] http://www.berzinarchives.com/web/en/archives/sutra/level3_lojong_material/general/hand_fear.html.

35. **Lewis, Michael.** *The Big Short.* New Yort : W. W. Norton & Company, 2010. 978-0393072235.

36. **Achenbach, Joel and Fahrenthold, David A.** Oil spill dumped 4.9 million barrels into Gulf of Mexico, latest measure shows. *The Washington Post.* Tuesday, 2010, August 3.

37. **Gay, Mara.** Scientists Have Sinking Feeling About Gulf Oil. *AOL News.* September, 2010, 13.

38. **Gascoigne, Bamber.** History of the Mongols. *History World.net.* [Online] 2001. [Cited: December 7, 2010.] http://www.historyworld. net/wrldhis/PlainTextHistories.asp?historyid=aa76.

39. Genghis Khan Featured Biography. *Biography.com.* [Online] 2010. [Cited: December 8, 2010.] http://www.biography.com/ genghis-khan/.

40. Anatomy of a Black Hole. *Expo/Science & Industry/Spacetime Wrinkles.* [Online] 1995. [Cited: December 8, 2010.] http://archive. ncsa.illinois.edu/Cyberia/NumRel/BlackHoleAnat.html.

41. **Miles, Jack.** *God: A Biography.* New York : Vintage, 1996. 978-0679743682.

42. **American Montessori Society.** What is Montessori? *American Montessori Society.* [Online] AMS, August 06, 2010. [Cited: August 06, 2010.] http://www.amshq.org/montessori.htm.

43. *Evaluating Montessori Education.* **Lillard, Angeline and Else-Quest, Nicole.** September 29th, s.l. : AAAS- Science, 2006, Vol. 313.

44. **Walker, Evan Harris.** *The physics of Consciousness.* Cambridge, MA : Basic Books: A Perseus Books Group, 2000. 978-0-7382-0436-9.

45. **Radin, Dean.** *The Consious Universe: The scientific truth of psychic phenomena.* New York : Harper Collins Publishers, 1997. 0-06-251502-0.

46. **Princeton Engineering Anomalies Research (PEAR).** PEAR Publications. *Princeton Engineering Anomalies Research: Scientific Study of Consciousness-Related Physical Phenomena.* [Online] Princeton University, September 2009. [Cited: August 12, 2010.] http://www.princeton.edu/~pear/publications.html.

47. **Murphy, Martha J.** Explorations in the use of group meditation

with persons in psychotherapy. *Dissertation.* San Francisco : California School of Professional Psychology, 1971.

48. **Mills, Randell L.** *The Grand Unified Theory of Classical Quantum Mechanics.* Ephrata, PA : Cadmus Professional Communications - Science Press Division, 2006. 0963517171.

49. *Physicists spooked by faster-than-light information transfer.* **Salart, D., et al.** August 14, NY : Nature, 2008, Vol. 454.

50. **Gauthier, Daniel J.** Superluminal Communication in Quantum Mechanics. [book auth.] Daniel Greenberger, Klaus Hentschel and Friedel Weinert. *Compendium of Quantum Physics.* Berlin Heidelberg : Springer-Verlag, 2009.

51. *Space Time Relaying versus Information Causality.* **Jacquet, Philipe.** Javier 25, Le Chesnay Cedex : Unite de recherche INRIA Rocquencourt, 2008, Vol. 2. 0249-6399.

52. **Debold, Elizabeth.** Field Work at the Frontier of Consciousness. *Elighten Next.* Spring/Summer, 2010, 46.

53. *Intuition through time: what does the seer see?* **Radin, D and Borges, A.** 4 (July), NY : Explore, 2009, Vol. 5.

54. **Haisch, Bernard.** *The God Theory.* San Francisco, CA : Weiser Books, 2006. 1-57863-374-5.

55. **Hawking, Stephen and Mlodinow, Leonard.** *The Grand Design.* s.l. : Bantum, 2010. 978-0553805376.

56. **Bushberg, Jerrold T., et al.** *The Essential Physics of Medical Imaging.* 2nd Edition. Sacramento : Lippincott Williams & Wilkins, 2001. p. 960. 978-0683301182.

57. **Lewin, Roger.** *Complexity: Life at the edge of chaos.* Chicago, Il : University of Chicago Press, 1999. 0-226-47655-3.

58. **Wolfram, Stephen.** *A New Kind of Science.* Champaine, Il : Stephen Wolfram LLC, 2002. 1-57955-008-8.

59. **International Organization for Standardization.** Information technology--Coding of audio-visual objects--Part 3: Audio. *International Organization for Standardization.* [Online] Revised 2009. [Cited: Aug 2, 2011.] http://www.iso.org/iso/iso_catalogue/catalogue_tc/catalogue_detail.htm?csnumber=42739. ISO/IEC 14496-3:2005.

60. **Gleick, James.** *Chaos: Making a new science.* New York : Viking Penguin Inc., 1987. 0140092501.

61. **Holland, John H.** *Emergence: From Chaos to Order.* Cambridge, Massachusettes : Perseus Books, 1998. 0-7382-0142-1.

62. **Holland, John H.** *Hidden Order: How Adaptation Builds Complexity.* Cambridge, Massachusettes : Perseus Books, 1995. 0-201-44230-2.

63. **Morowitz, Harold J.** *The Emergence of Everything.* New York : Oxford University Press, 2002. 0-19-513513-X.

64. **Moorton, Richard F.** Hesiod as Precursor to the Presocratic Philosophers: A Voeglinian View. *Louisiana State University.* [Online] 2001. [Cited: 12 04, 2008.] http://www.lsu.edu/.

65. **Ashliman, D.L.** Thor and Midgard Serpent. *University of Pittsburgh.* [Online] 05 12, 1997. [Cited: August 17, 2010.] http://www.pitt.edu/~dash/thorserpent.html.

66. **Clifford, Richard J.** Creation and Destruction: A Reappraisal of the Chaoskampf Theory in the Old Testament. *The Catholic Biblical Quarterly.* 2007.

67. **Campbell, Joseph.** *The Masks of God, Volume I.* New York : Penguin, 1991. ISBN-13: 978-0140194432.

68. **Radin, Dean, et al.** Double-Blind Test of the Effects of Distant Intention on Water Crystal Formation. *Journal Explore.* September/October, 2006, Vol. 2, 5.

69. **Ge, Z M, et al.** Non-Linear Dynamics and Chaos Control of a damped satellite with partially-filled liquid. *Journal of Sound and Vibration.* Novermber 12, 1998, Vol. 217, 5.

70. *Gaia Again.* **Karnania, Mahesh and Annilaa, Arto.** 1, Dublin : Elsivier Ireland, 2009, Vol. 95. doi:10.1016/j.biosystems.2008.07.003.

71. **Hodges, Andrew.** *Alan Turing: the Enigma.* New York : Walker and Company, 2000. 0-8027-7580-2.

72. **Falcke, Heino, et al.** Astroparticle Physics with LOPES and LOFAR. Nijmegen, The Netherlands : ASTRON, Dwingeloo, The Netherlands; University of Nijmegen, The Netherlands; MPIfR Bonn; LOPES & KASCADE Grande Collaboration, 2010.

73. *The speed of quantum information and the preferred frame: analysis of experimental data.* **Scarani, Valerio, et al.** 276, s.l. : Quantum Physics Letters A, Elsivier, October 30, 2008, Physics Letters A, Vol. 1, pp. 1-7. 10.1016/S0375-9601(00)00609-5.

74. **Lanza, Robert and Berman, Bob.** *Biocentrism.* Dallas, TX : Benbella Books, Inc., 2009. 978-1935251-74-3.

75. **Choi, Charles Q.** Spooky Eyes: Using Human Volunteers to Witness Quantum Entanglement. *Scientific American.* 2010, June 3rd.

76. *Entangled Mechanical Oscillators.* **Jost, J D, et al.** quant-ph, Boulder CO : National Institute of Standards and Technology, January 29, 2009, Vol. 1. arXiv:0901.4779v1.

77. *Energy-Entanglement Relation for Quantum Energy Teleportation.* **Hotta, Masahiro.** June 25, Tokyo Japan : Quantum Physics, 2010, Vol. Submitted . arXiv:1002.0200v2.

78. **Seife, Charles.** Spooky Action' Passes a Relativistic Test. *Science.* March, 2000, Vol. 287, 5460.

79. **Radin, Dean and Schlitz, M. J.** Gut feelings, intuition, and emotions: An exploratory study. *Journal of Alternative and Complementary Medicine.* 11, 2005, Vol. 4.

80. **Hameroff, Stuart and Penrose, Roger.** Orchestrated reduction of quantum coherence in brain microtubules: A model for consciousness. *Mathematics and Computers in Simulation.* April, 1996, Vol. 40, 3-4.

81. **Mavromatos, Nick E., Mershin, Andreas and Nanopoulos, Dimitri V.** QED-Cavity model of microtubules implies dissipationless energy transfer and biological quantum teleportation. *International Journal of Modern Physics B.* 2002, Vol. 16, 24, pp. p3623-3642.

82. **Ostrowski, Marcin.** Minimum energy required to copy one bit of information. *Cornell University Library.* [Online] 2010. http://arxiv.org/abs/1004.4732v2. arXiv:1004.4732v2 [cs.IT].

83. *Quantum information processing: The case of vanishing interaction energy.* **Dugic, Miroljub and Cirkovic, Milan M.** 291, s.l. : Elsevier, Oct 27th, 2002, Journal Ref. Phys. Lett. A, Vol. 302. arXiv:quant-ph/0210186v1.

84. **Vaccaro, Joan A. and Barnett, Stephen M.** Cornell University Library. *arxiv.org.* [Online] 1, April 29th, 2010. [Cited: April 29th, 2011.] http://arxiv.org/abs/1004.5330v1. arXiv:1004.53330v1.

85. **Ostrowski, Marcin.** Cornell University Library. *Cornell University.* [Online] January 18th, 2011. [Cited: April 29th, 2011.] http://arxiv.org/abs/1101.3070v1. arXiv:1101.3070v1 [physics. pop-ph].

86. **Weber, Bruce H. and Depew, David J.** *Evolution and Learning: The Baldwin Effect Reconsidered.* Boston, MA : MIT Press, 2003. ISBN 0-262-23229-4.

87. **Popper, Karl.** Natural Selection and the Emergence of Mind. *Dialectica.* No 3, 1978, Vol. 32, 4.

88. **Mainzer, Klaus.** The emergence of mind and brain: an evolutionary, computational, and philosophical approach. *Progress in Brain Research.* December 31, 2007, Vol. 168, pp. 115-132.

89. **The American Thanks-Giving Foundation.** Gratitude. *Thanks-Giving Square.* [Online] Thanks-Giving Foundation, 2007. [Cited: September 10, 2010.] http://www.thanksgiving.org/usa.html.

90. **Miami, University of.** Overfishing Large Sharks Impacts Entire Marine Ecosystem, Shrinks Shellfish Supply. *ScienceDaily.* [Online] 29 March, 2007. [Cited: April 29th, 2011.] http://www.sciencedaily. com/releases/2007/03/070329145922.htm.

91. **Dowd, Allan.** *World pays high price for overfishing, studies say.* [News Article] [ed.] Peter Galloway. Vancouver, CA, BC, CA : Thomson Reuters, Sep 14, 2010. Reuters.

92. **Eckhart, Tolle.** *The Power of Now: A Guide to Spiritual Enlightenment.* Novato, CA : New World Library, 1999. 978-1577311522.

93. *Mental Training Affects Distribution of Limited Brain Resources.* **Slagter, HA, et al.** 6, s.l. : PLoS Biology, 2007, Vol. 5. e138. doi:10.1371/ journal.pbio.0050138.

94. *Regulation of the nerual circuitry of emotion by compassion meditation: effects of meditative expertise.* **Lutz, A, et al.** s.l. : PLoS ONE, 2008, Vol. May.

95. **Wicks, Robert.** Arthur Schopenhauer. *Stanford Encyclopedia of*

Philosophy. [Online] Stanford University, 11 17, 2007. [Cited: 09 20, 2010.] http://plato.stanford.edu/entries/schopenhauer/.

96. **Tolle, Eckhart.** *Stillness Speaks.* Novato, CA : New World Library, 2003. 978-1577314004.

97. **Pigliucci, Massimo.** Science and Fundamentalism: A strategy on how to deal with anti-science fundamentalism. *EMBO Reports.* May 2005, Vol. 12, 6, pp. 1106 - 1109.

98. **Cartilage, Edwin.** Penrose claims to have glimpsed universe before Big. *physicsworld.com.* [Online] November 19, 2010. [Cited: November 19, 2010.] http://physicsworld.com/cws/article/news/44388.

99. **Tang, Xiao, et al.** *High Speed Fiber-Based Quantum Key Distribution using Polarization Encoding.* Gaithersburg, MD : National Institute of Standards and Technology (NIST), 2005.

100. *The Einstein-Podolsky-Rosen Paradox in the Brain: The Transferred Potential.* **Grinberg-Zylberbaum, J., et al.** 4, 1994, Physics Essays, Vol. 7, pp. 422-428.

101. **Radin, Dean.** *Entangled Minds.* NY : Paraview Pocket Books, 2006. 978-1-4165-1677-4.

102. **Bhaumik, Mani.** *Code Name God: The Spiritual Odyssey of a Man of Science.* NY : The Crossroad Publishing Company, 2005. 978-0824522810.

103. **Sheldrake, Rupert.** *Morphic Resonance: The nature of Formative Causation.* Rochester, VT : Park Street Press, 2009. 978-1-59477-317-4.

104. **Goodwin, Liz.** Stephen Hawking says afterlife is a fairy story. [Online] May 16, 2011. [Cited: 05 16, 2011.] http://news.yahoo.com/s/yblog_thelookout/20110516/us_yblog_thelookout/stephen-hawking-says-afterlife-is-a-fairy-story/print.

105. **Sample, Ian.** Stephen Hawking: 'there is no heaven; it's a fairy story'. *Guardian.co.uk.* [Online] May 15, 2011. [Cited: May 16, 2011.] http://www.guardian.co.uk/science/2011/may/15/stephen-hawking-interview-there-is-no-heaven.

106. **Bosveld, Jane.** Will natural science pin down our supernatural

essence? *DISCOVER Magazine.* June, 2007, Soul Search- Mind & Brain.

107. **Blanke, Olaf and Arzy, Shahar.** The Out-of-Body Experience: Disturbed Self-Processing at the Temporo-Parietal Junction. *The Neuroscientist.* 2005, Vol. 11, 1.

108. **Carter, Chris.** *Science and the Near-Death Experience: How Consciousness Survives Death.* Rochester, Vermont : Inner Traditions, 2010. 978-1594773563.

109. **Mannucci, Mark.** *Moment of Death.* National Geographic, 2008.

110. **Stevenson, Ian.** *Twenty Cases suggestive of Reincarnation.* s.l. : University of Virginia Press, 1980. 978-0813908724.

111. **Tucker, Jim B.** *Life Before Life: A Scienctific Investigation of Children's Memories of Previous Lives.* New York : St. Martin's Press, 2005. 978-0312321376.

INDEX

A

B

F

G

N

O

P

Quran 4, 71

R

Ra 48, 57
Radiation Therapy 96
Radin, Dean 176, 178, 179, 181
Random 69, 70, 79, 86, 92, 100–105, 112, 124
Random Number generator (RNG) 91
Reality xiv, 6, 12, 31, 36, 43, 45, 48, 49, 50, 52, 53, 55, 73, 75, 79, 80, 84,
      88–93, 103, 110, 118–120, 123, 126, 130, 142, 146, 147, 151
Red giants 57
Redundancy 158, 162
Reincarnation 160, 168, 182
Relative State Interpretation 79
Relativity xiii, 6, 83, 84, 85, 87, 123, 158–160
Religion ix, x, 1–5, 11, 15, 16, 19, 20, 22, 28, 30, 31, 33, 44, 51, 58, 68,
      70, 72–74, 91, 99, 136, 143, 144, 151, 152, 155, 164, 173, 175
Research xii, 6, 8, 9, 14–16, 23, 65, 70, 80–82, 85, 92, 99, 102, 108, 114,
      123, 127–129, 145, 150, 154, 157, 160, 162, 165, 174–176, 180
Responsibility xii, 20, 33, 47, 54, 115, 134, 135
Resurrection 43
Roosevelt, Franklin D. 5
Rules 1, 4–6, 10, 14, 19, 26, 30, 34, 36, 75, 84, 85, 87, 97, 98, 100, 112,
      113, 117, 134, 147, 148, 164
Rutan, Burt 47
Rwanda 21, 175

S

Santa Fe Institute 97, 134
Satori 90
Schlitz, Marilyn 85
Schopenhauer, Arthur 14, 144, 180
Schrödinger, Erwin 78
Science ix, x, xiv, 2, 6, 12, 17, 24, 35, 38, 47, 56, 57, 60, 61, 63, 66, 68,
      70, 77–79, 82, 83, 85, 86, 91–93, 96, 97, 99, 100, 104, 105, 110,
      114, 117, 119, 122, 123, 130, 134, 135, 151–155, 156, 159, 160,
      162, 164, 167, 169, 173, 175–179, 181, 182
Scientific American 122, 179
Second Law of Thermodynamics 129
Shangdi 26
Shantideva 40
Sheldrake, Rupert 163, 181
Śhiva 54, 55, 58
Sidereus Nuncius 30, 175